Man
on a
Mission

10/13

Other Books in the Zonderkidz Biography Series

Man on a Mission

the
David Hilmers
Story

Dr. David Hilmers
with Rick Houston

ZONDERVAN.com/
AUTHORTRACKER
follow your favorite authors

We want to hear from you. Please send your comments about this book to us in care of zreview@zondervan.com. Thank you.

ZONDERKIDZ

Man on a Mission
Copyright © 2013 by Dr. David Hilmers with Rick Houston

This title is also available as a Zondervan ebook.
Visit www.zondervan.com/ebooks.

Requests for information should be addressed to:
Zonderkidz, 5300 Patterson Ave SE, Grand Rapids, Michigan 49530

Library of Congress Cataloging-in-Publication Data

Hilmers, David, 1950-
     Man on a mission : the David Hilmers story / Dr. David Hilmers with Rick Houston.
          pages cm
     Includes bibliographical references and index.
     Audience: Ages 9-12.
     ISBN 978-0-310-73613-4 (alk. paper)
     1. Hilmers, David, 1950s—Juvenile literature. 2. Astronautss—United States—Biographys—Juvenile literature. 3. Physicianss—United States—Biographys—Juvenile literature. 4. Disaster reliefs—Juvenile literature. I. Houston, Rick, 1967- II. Title.
     TL789.85.H55A3 2013
     629.450092s—dc23
     [B]   2013005447

Cover design: Mark Veldheer
Cover photography: NASA
Interior design: Ben Fetterley, Greg Johnson/Textbook Perfect

Printed in the United States of America

13 14 15 16 17 18 / DCI / 20 19 18 17 16 15 14 13 12 11 10 9 8 7 6 5 4 3

Contents

Chapter 1

Just Another Sunset

The announcer counted down the seconds to the launch of STS-51J, the first of my four flights on board the space shuttle.

T-minus twelve ...
Eleven ...
Ten ...
And go for main engine start ...
T-minus six ...
We have main engine start ...

Just past 11:15 a.m. on October 3, 1985, I was strapped into my seat on the flight deck of the brand-new shuttle *Atlantis*. Outside, it was sunny and warm in Florida at the Kennedy Space Center (KSC). Inside the shuttle, somewhere far below my seat, the fuse on the three main engines was lit, and the engines roared to life.

I'd been preparing for this moment for months, but I was not expecting so much noise and vibration. Maybe I shouldn't have been surprised. After all, the engines provided a total thrust of more than 1.2 million pounds, and when combined with the power provided by the solid rocket boosters (SRBs), was enough to get my four crewmates and me into orbit.

Four . . .
Three . . .
Two . . .
One . . .
Ignition and liftoff!

If the lighting of the main engines shook things up, the ignition of the twin solid rocket boosters was something else altogether. The SRBs were located on either side of the big, burnt-orange external tank to which *Atlantis* was attached. Huge plumes of steam and smoke around the launch pad let observers know the boosters had fired. Inside the shuttle, the crew and I knew the SRBs had started from the slow but unmistakable release from the ground.

I had been through many training sessions that simulated the motion of launch, but they didn't do justice to the actual experience. The sensation of being catapulted off the launch pad that I had expected was not there. Instead, it was replaced by a very loud roar and a shaking and rattling that completely enveloped us as we rumbled off the launch pad.

Was this much vibration normal? Surely not! The shuttle was holding together . . . for now. A sense of helplessness washed over me, because at this point, I was just

Takeoff of the *Atlantis*.

along for the ride. There was little I could do if anything went wrong.

The doubts passed quickly. This was the twenty-first flight of the space shuttle program, and every other mission up until then had launched and landed safely. That meant that the National Aeronautics and Space Administration—NASA, for short—had things completely figured out, right?

A little less than four months after this, my first launch, the loss of *Challenger* and her seven-person crew showed all of us just how wrong we were.

But that tragedy was still in the future, as I lay there, pressed into my seat, right behind the pilot, Ron Grabe. To my immediate left was fellow mission specialist and flight engineer Bob Stewart. In front of Bob was the mission commander, Bo Bobko, while seated alone downstairs on the mid-deck was payload specialist Bill Pailes.

We were off to the races.

About two minutes into the flight, the spent SRBs separated with a noisy thump. With "SRBs sep" came a much smoother ride, but also a gradual buildup of g-forces due to our continued acceleration. Although it was not an uncomfortable sensation, the increased pressure on our chests made it a bit harder to breathe and talk. The next six minutes were spent listening for various milestones during our ascent. Finally, at about eight and a half minutes, the three main engines stopped. Suddenly we went from feeling three g's to none. I was more than 250 miles above the surface of Earth in space, traveling 17,500 mph—just short of five miles per second.

As my body adjusted to weightlessness, I felt a little like a clumsy young colt taking its first tentative steps. I unstrapped the safety harnesses that bound me to my seat and floated toward one of the windows as *Atlantis* sailed high over the coast of Africa, unprepared for the incredible view that unfolded right before my eyes. I had seen sunsets many times from ground level, yet this one was something so much more beautiful. The colors were brighter and more vivid than I ever could have imagined. I was stunned by the majestic splendor.

Courtesy of NASA

Crew of the STS-51J mission.

I mentioned it to Bo, who had flown on board the space shuttle twice before, and I'll never forget his reaction. *Oh, that's just another sunset.*

Nearly thirty years have passed since I made my way to that window, giving me plenty of time to reflect on what the view meant to me. This was so far outside anything I had ever experienced. God had created this awesome vista. Our home planet is something far bigger than the tiny sliver in which we live every day, yet at the same time, Mother Earth is just another rock bobbing around in a vast universe that God also created. The view from the window that day gave me an all-new perspective on the world and my place in it. I became aware of just how small I really am, and how big God was, is, and always will be.

There I was, floating in space, drifting this way and that in the weightlessness of the *Atlantis* crew module, thinking about how some desperately poor and ravaged areas on Earth appeared lovely from high above. Why should these areas be home to so much suffering? I had what amounted to a doctorate in electrical engineering. I had been a naval flight officer in the Marines. I was an astronaut aboard the space shuttle. And while those qualifications had been very useful in the military and at NASA, they weren't of much value to a sick or starving child.

Funny, it took my launching into space to help me launch a new career. The majesty of what I saw helped clarify a course of action that I had long considered. I wanted to be a doctor. Although I had seriously considered applying to medical school while serving in the Marine Corps nearly a decade earlier, the timing wasn't quite right. After that, I wound up in Houston as a brand-new astronaut.

As I was floating hundreds of miles above Earth, an idea began to take hold. If I returned from the flight and pursued the life of a physician, I now could use my talents to help others I couldn't even see as they lived out their lives on the small blue planet that appeared so beautiful below through the space shuttle window.

As a doctor, I could make a difference. It took more than a decade—I wasn't finished flying in space just yet!—but I was eventually able to live out that dream.

Chapter 2

Midwest Moderation

For as long as I can remember, hard work and curiosity have been a part of my life.

My grandfather drowned during the depths of the Great Depression when my father, Paul Hilmers, was just thirteen years old or so. For better or worse, that made Dad the man of the house and he eventually took over the greenhouse that my grandparents had established in the 1920s on the outskirts of the small town of DeWitt, Iowa. During World War II, he served as a military policeman who guarded German prisoners in France.

His was a work ethic that he began instilling in me not long after I was born on January 28, 1950, in nearby Clinton. Although my father was not a highly educated man on paper, he was one of the most inquisitive people I've ever known. When a problem needed solving, he could be very creative in working out a solution. If he thought of a better way to do something, he wasn't afraid to try it.

Because he loved to experiment with all kinds of different crops, we had greenhouses and orchards, gardens and vineyards, and probably an acre of corn and flowers all over the place. Our house—home to myself, Dad, my mother, Matilda, and sister, Virginia—sat on one small portion of the property. Of course, Dad built it.

Paul Hilmers took being a jack-of-all-trades to new heights. He ran the greenhouse business by himself. He was a deliveryman and made whatever repairs needed to be made. Many times, I was laboring right there beside him, watching and learning. In fact, I'm fairly certain I still have my first paycheck somewhere in my files—I was maybe five years old, and received the grand sum of $1 for a day's work with my trusty miniature wheelbarrow.

Because Dad had so much responsibility resting on his shoulders, the work could be difficult and at times almost brutal. We had a furnace that was used to warm the greenhouses during the winter, and he would often sleep close to it so he could shovel coal into the hopper overnight. Between growing seasons, fresh dirt for the greenhouses was taken inside, load after load after load, and piled into long, raised benches. Next came fertilizer and perlite—small pellets of volcanic glass often used to condition soil—and we mixed it all together, chopping and kneading it with hoes. Whether it was blazing hot or bone-numbing cold, the work had to continue.

Out of sheer necessity, my father rarely if ever sat still. Looking back, I can see where I have picked up from

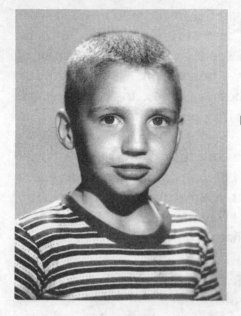

Me in fifth grade.

my father that same kind of—what's the best word for it?—restlessness. I was in the Marines, and then I was an astronaut. There was more out there left to do following my NASA career, so I went to medical school and became a physician.

Then, after achieving my lifelong dream of becoming a doctor, I wound up being an academic physician and researcher and working in the mission field as well. I've been on many trips over the years, and after a few months at home, I'll begin to plan when and where my next one will take place. Each and every step has purpose—it has to be worthwhile. When I look back on a workweek, I want to know that I have been a good steward and have spent my time wisely.

Thankfully, I also had the freedom to be a kid when I finished my chores. There were woods near our home, and my friends and I spent many an hour exploring them. We played and we hunted, but we never got into any serious trouble. There was a line to be crossed, and we knew full well what the consequences would be if we stepped over it.

I remember having a collection of *everything*—butterflies, rocks, coins, and baseball cards. There was once a Babe Ruth card in my treasure trove of knickknacks, but it probably was traded away for some silly little thing.

Who knows what that card might be worth today!

—◄ ►—

My father was a very ethical man and did many things out of a definite sense of right and wrong, and I admired him greatly for that. But one area in which we did not see eye to eye, especially as I became an adult and grew stronger in my own faith, was religion.

My dad lived essentially two lives when it came to his beliefs. When I was young, he was, for all intents and purposes, an agnostic—someone who doubts the existence of God. Later in his life, Dad became an atheist—someone who does not believe in God, period. He was basically anti-religion and not very supportive of some of the things I was doing for the church. That was hard for me to take sometimes, especially coming from a man whom I otherwise respected so dearly.

Mom made sure that we went to Sunday school and church, and while the congregation was made up of caring people who looked after each other, there wasn't a lot of open expression of their faith. Maybe that was due to the moderation often exhibited by people from the Midwest, whose behavior isn't likely to swing from one extreme to the other. People tended to adhere to the expected norms, right down the middle of the road, or else someone might think them strange.

Midwesterners are wonderful. We didn't lock our doors at night, because crime didn't really exist. Everybody knew everybody else, and most everyone trusted each other. And if you weren't trustworthy, people knew that too. Life in our particular small town was idyllic, almost like something out of *The Andy Griffith Show*. But when it came to messages of faith, controversy was avoided. Sunday mornings, we were told to "do good," and not so much about sin and the need for a personal Savior.

My faith journey was just getting started.

As it was for so many kids, school was an awkward period of my life. I was a good student and relatively intelligent, but at that point in my life, I didn't really want anyone to know it. There are a lot of hurtful labels that often get hung on smart kids—*geek, nerd, bookworm, egghead*, take your pick—and I wanted no part of any of them.

So I threw myself into sports, playing football and basketball and running track. As "cool" as it might have seemed to be an athlete, I still wasn't very outgoing. Worse yet, I was very, very shy around girls. I could be wrong here, but I might have had one date while I was in high school. Think about that one for a second. I would one day become what some people might consider a dashing aviator in the Marine Corps and a NASA astronaut, but still, I sat at home alone on prom night in high school.

I was the valedictorian of Central Community High School when I graduated in 1968, but I don't know that I ever truly applied myself to my studies until I was in the Naval Postgraduate School a decade later. I was diligent in school, but only to a point, because I never felt pushed or challenged. I didn't *have* to study very much.

My parents would have been deeply disappointed if I hadn't continued my education, and there really was no discussion about this; I headed off to college.

Chapter 3

College Life, Poison Ivy, and a Choice

Cornell College is a very small private liberal arts school in Mount Vernon, Iowa, less than seventy miles from where I grew up in DeWitt. Its alumni include several congressmen, the founder of Goodwill Industries, a Pulitzer Prize winner, an Emmy Award–winning actor, and an author or two.

And one astronaut.

Just like high school, college turned out to be a rather confusing experience. I double majored in economics and math, when, in my heart of hearts, I actually wanted to become a doctor. The dream was suppressed by my father's advice that math/econ would be a useful major, a distinct lack of focus that was probably compounded by sports and a newfound social life. I didn't get out and about much in high school, but when I packed my bags for college, I became much more socially outgoing.

Football was one of the many sports in which I participated.

I continued to play football and run track in college, but because I thought it might be a cooler sport, I also walked onto Cornell's wrestling team as a sophomore. It wasn't that I was trying to make a ragtag squad of misfits, either. The Rams of Cornell have won several individual wrestling titles over the years, and more than sixty have been named NCAA All-Americans. Some have been enshrined in the National Wrestling Hall of Fame, and some have gone to the Olympics. It's almost unheard of to start playing any sport at the college level, and especially one that was as successful as Cornell's program.

That first year, it seemed like my primary responsibility on the team was to get beat up a lot! Improvement came little by little, but not to the point where I was ever considered a superstar. My senior year, however, we did win the conference team championship. The sport taught me important lessons in humility and tenacity. Not being afraid to attempt something new would become a recurring theme in my life. Like, for instance, the Marines, NASA, and medicine.

The work ethic instilled in me from an early age by my father, however, was never far away. School cost money and part of my scholarship was a work grant. After going to football, track, or wrestling practice, I would change clothes and either wait tables at the school "Commons," where all the students ate together, or wash dishes afterward if practice ran late. On Saturdays, it was a tradition at the school to have steak for dinner. I would finish a football game, wrestling match, or track meet, and then hustle to the grill, where I would cook the steaks. It was not unusual for me to wolf down a couple, particularly if I had just spent the week starving myself to make weight for a wrestling match.

—◀ ▶—

The Vietnam War was at its peak when I entered college in the fall of 1968, and protests were so rampant that a group of demonstrators briefly took over Cornell's administration building at one point. In 1969, my lottery number came up for the draft. I really had no idea what I was going to do after college, the dream of attending medical school having been temporarily sidetracked. The reality of deciding what I wanted to do when I grew up came a year or so later when my longtime college girlfriend decided to end our relationship for someone else.

Little did I know that these events were pushing me toward a career in the military. Walking into my dorm one day near the end of my junior year at Cornell, I noticed a brochure on the floor advertising the Marines' Platoon Leaders Class (PLC). I picked it up and immediately called a recruiter. Within days, I was on a bus to Des Moines, Iowa, for my physical. Once I enrolled in the PLC program in April 1971, I headed off to Quantico, Virginia, for basic training that summer.

Marine Corps Base Quantico can be an intimidating place, and for me, I lived in almost total fear for the first few weeks I was there. Once, we had to pitch tents in the middle of the woods. When the drill instructor pointed toward where he thought mine was supposed to go, I noticed a problem and tried to protest.

But, Drill Instructor, sir, that's all poison ivy.

He let me have it. In no uncertain terms, I was informed that I would pitch my tent when the drill instructor told me to pitch it, how he told me to pitch it, and, most importantly, *where* he told me to pitch it. So

My early days in the Marines.

up went my tent, and a day or two later my whole body was covered in blisters from where I'd broken out in a terrible rash. Never in my life had I been so completely miserable, and it evidently showed. When a Navy doctor happened to pass by in the mess hall, he took one look and immediately ordered me to report to the infirmary for treatment.

Still, about halfway through basic training, I finally realized that my superiors weren't actually trying to kill me and that I was really going to survive what seemed like a very bad dream. After completing the course that summer, I went back to Cornell for my senior year. It might not have been the direction that I had planned on taking when I entered college, but a commission as a second lieutenant in the United States Marine Corps was waiting for me when I graduated *summa cum laude* in the spring of 1972.

The Marines were just getting started honing young David Hilmers. Almost as soon as I could stash my cap and gown somewhere, I was back at Quantico for The Basic School—a six-month course where all new Marine officers are sent to further craft their leadership skills. There were 250 or so of us; a good number were recent graduates of the United States Naval Academy in Annapolis, Maryland. I was ranked first in my class, and as the course neared its conclusion in late 1972, we had the opportunity to choose a military occupational specialty—essentially, what our jobs would be. Computers were the hot new thing at the time, so I requested data processing. There were no openings available.

Okay, so maybe I'll try flight school.

Really, not much more planning and forethought went into the decision than just that. *Okay, so maybe I'll try flight school.* It's hard to fathom the direction that this one thought would eventually lead me. Come to think of it, that season of my life seems to have been one "if-then" proposition right after another.

If I had been a little more focused, *then* I might have become a doctor more than twenty years earlier than when I eventually did.

If I had not been jilted by my girlfriend and been open to reading that Marine Corps brochure on the floor of the dorm, *then* I probably would have been drafted into who knows what branch of the military or might even have gotten an exemption.

If the data processing job had been open at the end of The Basic School, *then* I wouldn't have become an aviator in the Marine Corps.

If I hadn't become an aviator in the Marine Corps, *then* I wouldn't have become an astronaut.

The beauty of it all is that despite my fumbling, God knew exactly what was best for me and my life. He worked it out for his purpose and glory, despite the fact that my life almost certainly would have turned out much differently had I entered medical school in my twenties. He knew what he was doing ... I just had to get out of the way.

Chapter 4

I Dare You

I had never been on an airplane when I left Iowa for boot camp back in April of 1971, but I was about to make up for it big-time.

Because my eyesight wasn't quite good enough, I trained to become a naval flight officer rather than a pilot. That was fine with me, because, if you'll remember, this wasn't something that had been a lifelong dream of mine. If my superiors wanted me to learn all there was to learn about targeting ordinance and figuring out how to get there in one of our multimillion-dollar aircraft, then that's exactly what I was going to do.

Learning such skills, and then putting them into practice, was very much like emergency-room medicine would one day become for me. Certain things had to get done by a certain time, or we would fly right over and miss the target. The same kind of urgency exists in the ER. You only get one chance to do it right, and you practice over and over and over again, readying yourself to perform under stress.

Flying itself came rather naturally to me. All that concerned me was doing the best job I possibly could. Maybe I was just young and dumb, but not even the very real dangers that were involved seemed to faze me. If somebody wanted to fly low to the deck, even less than a hundred feet or so, so be it. Bring it on. I loved the acrobatics that our jet fighters could handle with ease. When I strapped into my seat, it didn't matter what we did—I never got sick.

Because of some experiences I'd been through in college, I felt a need to quiet small doubts that sometimes cropped up. I wasn't a rich kid from the big city, my family was not influential, and I always wondered whether that had played a role in the disappointments that I had experienced. I really wanted to show myself that I could be the very best at whatever I tried to do and I tried to do my best in all my training courses. That same kind of drive in others can sometimes tend to get rather ugly. They'll stop at nothing to make it to the top, caring little or nothing about whom they have to claw their way over, under, around, or through.

My hope is that I was never perceived that way. I wanted to do well, but not at the expense of someone else. I was competitive, yes, but only to take away the clouds of doubt in my heart and to see how far I could push myself.

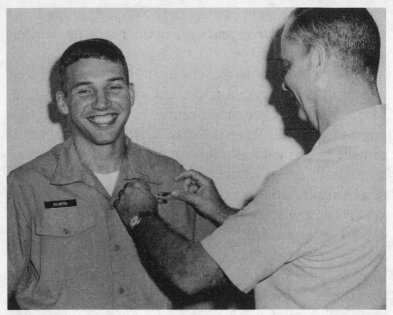

Receiving my wings.

As much as I was learning in flight training, another area of my life was beginning to develop in ways that were every bit as exciting. The faith that I had grown up with was challenged in a very real and very deep way during a series of meetings with a man from an evangelical group called the Navigators. Deep down, what did I really believe about Jesus and the Bible? Was it just something to pass the time away on Sunday mornings?

No. It wasn't. Over the course of the next few weeks and months, it began to dawn on me that faith in God could be a living and vibrant aspect of my life. It wasn't something to be tucked away in a box and put on a shelf, only to be taken down, dusted off, and used when it seemed convenient. Like any muscle, the convictions that were developing deep down inside me needed regular exercise. Along with Scripture, I began to read the works of Christian authors like C. S. Lewis. I hungered to learn about what I did not know.

More than anything else, however, I realized I was a sinner in need of salvation.

—◁▷—

After completing Naval Flight Officer School and receiving my wings in October 1973, I was assigned to the Marine Air Corps Station in Cherry Point, North Carolina. There, I went from flying in training aircraft to a state-of-the-art, modern combat aircraft. I was put into the cockpit of the A–6 Intruder, a low-flying and all-weather subsonic attack aircraft manufactured by Grumman Aerospace Corporation.

I found myself in a Marine Corps attack squadron, with a Marine battalion landing team, in the Mediterranean Sea, spending a year with the "grunts" of the infantry as a forward air controller, and later on station in Iwakuni, Japan, going places and meeting cultures this quiet Iowa farm boy would never otherwise have encountered. As hard as it was for me to believe, I was actually getting paid to go fly in these awesome jet aircraft and see places I'd never dreamed of.

That's not to say that there weren't a few close calls along the way. Still, the dangers did not matter. I was a Marine aviator, and that was going to look really good

An A-6 Intruder.

on an application to medical school. As it turned out, that's exactly what happened. It just took a little longer than I expected, because I was about to take an incredible detour to low Earth orbit.

Chapter 5

Dream Delayed ... for Now

In 1976, after returning from an overseas stint, I started to get serious about applying to med school. From where I was stationed at Cherry Point, I headed over to Chapel Hill to check out the University of North Carolina and to nearby Durham to see what Duke University might have to offer. The people I met there were nice enough, I suppose, but for whatever reason, they didn't exactly welcome me with open arms, either.

Another brush-off came in the form of a letter from Baylor College. It began by saying that my interest was appreciated, but then the hammer dropped. At twenty-six years of age, the writer informed me, I was probably a little too old to begin studying medicine. The note landed one final blow with a thinly veiled suggestion that I consider another career altogether.

Ouch. The ironic part of the story is that the letter came from Baylor College of Medicine in Houston, Texas, where I'm now on the faculty!

At least I could console myself with the fact that I had other options, and they were good ones. My wife, Lynn, whom I met after returning from basic training during my final year of college and married nearly three years later, gave birth to our first child, Matt, on September 28, 1976. Rather than continue to subject my growing family to the uncertainty of whether or not I would get into medical school, I applied for and was accepted into the prestigious Naval Postgraduate School in Monterey, California, to study electrical engineering. Not only was there no cost, I would actually continue to be paid by the Marines while I went about my studies.

The days of being able to do well in class without much effort seemed to be ancient history as I dug into the basic engineering courses that I needed to get under my belt before I started into the heavy graduate school courses at the Naval Postgraduate School. I mapped out a really aggressive program in which I would earn not only a master of science degree, but also what amounted to a doctorate in electrical engineering. And if that wasn't difficult enough, I would be doing it all in the span of about twenty-seven months beginning in the fall of 1976 and ending in early 1979.

For the first time in my life, I considered myself a serious student. I had done extremely well in the classroom for most of my life, but I'd also found time to be distracted by any number of things. At Monterey, I hunkered down and focused on studying harder than I ever had in my life. Not only was I more mature, but my drive to be the best continued to manifest itself. As a result, I pushed myself as hard as I could, took up to twenty-one hours of course credit at a time, and was able to graduate with my coveted degree of electrical engineer. If I'm not mistaken, I received just one grade as low as an A-minus on the way to being the top graduate in the class.

In case you were wondering, my dissertation was entitled "Spatial-Temporal Filter for Clutter Suppression and Target Detection of Real-World Infrared Images." Whew. I get tired now just reading the title. You should've seen me when I was actually writing it!

—◄ ►—

When NASA selected thirty-five new astronauts to be a part of the upcoming space shuttle program in 1978, I paid little or no attention to the announcement. I was up to my eyeballs in homework and diapers, and not only that, traveling in space had never really been on my radar screen anyway.

Another son, Dan, joined the family on August 10, 1979, while I was serving a tour of duty in Iwakuni, Japan. I was able to arrange a quick leave to head back to the States for Dan's grand entrance, and not long afterward, the family was able to join me in Japan. With two young children in tow, we were experiencing big changes in our home life. My career path was also about to make a dramatic turn, and one that I had never really considered an option.

Me with the boys on my 30th birthday.

As the commanding officer of a small unit, I was reading the morning bulletins one day when one in particular got my attention. The Marines were in the process of accepting nominations to forward on to NASA for another astronaut selection. The requirements were relatively straightforward. They were looking for people with bachelor's degrees.

Check.

Applicants also needed to have some sort of technical degree.

I was an electrical engineer.

Check.

Flight experience was a plus too.

Check.

Why not? I thought. Being an astronaut sounded more exciting than what I was doing right then, and I had a commitment of four more years in the Marines as a "payback" for graduate school, so I figured almost on the spot that I would give it a shot. Did I think I had a serious chance? No, not really, because I was sure there would be hundreds of more-qualified Marines who would want to throw their names in the hat. The odds, though, weren't going to stop me. It was almost like a game—I probably wasn't going to make the cut, but just how far *could* I get? I filled out an application, sent it in, and waited to see what might happen.

Chapter 6

Planes, Trains, Automobiles...
and the Space Shuttle

Five months.

That's how long it took to hear anything from NASA after all my paperwork had been filed, approved, and forwarded to the space agency by the Marines. I didn't really expect to be selected as an astronaut, but I figured I would at least hear *something*. A feeling washed over me that it wasn't going to happen, but instead of disappointment, there was a sense of peace. Satisfied that I had at least tried, I figured it just probably wasn't in God's plan for my life. I put it aside and went about my business.

Just a few days later, NASA contacted me and said to submit to a full physical exam.

After that took place, I was going to be among the sixth and final group of applicants to be interviewed for the upcoming astronaut candidate class. Out of nearly 3,500 submissions—585 for those who would actually fly the shuttle and 2,880 for the openings as mission specialists—121 of us were headed for Johnson Space Center (JSC) in Houston, Texas, for what amounted to astronaut tryouts. Although it was still a long shot, because fewer than twenty would eventually be selected, the door had just cracked open the tiniest bit.

That door, however, very nearly slammed in my face before I ever got to Houston. As soon as I could, I lined up a physical with the flight surgeon on the base in Japan. My eyesight had kept me from being a pilot in the Marines, and after my checkup, it appeared that it also might prevent me from joining NASA. It wasn't that I couldn't see without inch-thick glasses. I could, but it was "iffy" as to whether I could meet the standards for eyesight that NASA had set for mission specialists.

My suggestion that the flight surgeon pass me anyway fell on deaf ears. Instead, I had to visit an ophthalmologist in Tokyo, about five hours away by the *shinkansen* (bullet train). After I did everything I could to pass the test, he finally relented and gave me the thumbs-up. I was good to go, but by that time, another problem had cropped up. The timing had been cut so close, it was going to be nearly impossible to get word back to NASA that I had been medically "cleared" and that I would actually be coming to Houston. Weighing my options, I trudged back to the visiting officers' quarters in which I was staying while in Tokyo. Just as it started to sink in that maybe this wasn't going to happen after all, there was a knock on the door.

Standing there was a female Navy lieutenant who worked in the ophthalmologist's office that I had just visited. She'd heard that I was in the process of applying for the astronaut office and just wanted to introduce herself. Oh, and by the way, her mother — get this — worked in the medical office at NASA in Houston. My heart almost skipped a beat, the questions flying fast and furious.

She does?

Really?

Is there any way you can get word to her that I passed my medical exam, and have her tell the selection committee that I'm cleared to come to Houston for the interviews?

As incredulous as I must have seemed to her, Lt. Moore's response was just the opposite.

Sure. I'll just call her tonight.

Just like that, a seemingly insurmountable obstacle had been overcome.

It wasn't a coincidence that Lt. Moore happened by that night. Remember all those "if-then" moments that I've encountered over the course of my life? This was definitely one of those. *If* she hadn't introduced herself, *then* I almost certainly never would have made it to Houston in time for the interview. The implication is clear ... no interviews, no NASA, at least not for me.

The next couple of days were not just a whirlwind but an all-out tornado of activity to prepare for the trip back to the United States.

I left Tokyo and got back to the base in Iwakuni as fast as possible. My travel orders were cut and hasty arrangements were made for the family to join me back home later; and then I found a buddy to give me a return lift to Tokyo in an A–4 Skyhawk jet. I hopped on board a military flight for the ten-hour journey to Travis Air Force Base, took a bus over to the airport in nearby San Francisco, and then went on a commercial airplane from there to Houston.

I was jet-lagged to the nth degree when my feet finally hit the ground in Texas. Sleep, however, would have to wait, because almost as soon as I arrived, there was a meet-and-greet social affair scheduled. Exhausted almost to the point of walking around in a stupor, I shook hands at the reception with a gentleman and wondered if he was somebody important.

He wasn't just important. He was somebody really, *really* important, about as high on the NASA food chain as it was possible to get. It was *just* John Young—the *Apollo 16* moonwalker who was serving at the time as chief of the astronaut office! That meant that he would be playing a major role in determining whether or not I was about to become an astronaut myself. Not only that, but John was also just a year away from commanding the very first flight of the space shuttle program.

And I had not the faintest clue who he was.

—◄ ►—

John Young.

Although somebody along the line had handed me a welcome packet, I wasn't quite sure where I was supposed to be or when. I decided on the fly that I would play along, just happy to be there. For the next week, the twenty-one of us in the sixth group of applicants that year underwent all sorts of physical and psychological testing.

The tests weren't quite the routine portrayed in the movie *The Right Stuff*, but they were indeed close. A couple of psychiatrists played good cop, bad cop and peppered us with all kinds of questions designed to probe our personalities. To simulate a "rescue sphere" that would transfer astronauts between spacecraft in case of some sort of accident, we were zipped up in cloth bags for an hour or so. That might have been a problem for somebody who was claustrophobic, but not me. I curled up for a much-needed nap.

Nerves were never an issue that week, up to and including the infamous round of interviews. Many would-be astronauts dread the thought of sitting down in front of a group of incredibly accomplished people and answering highly detailed questions. A lot consider it to be the most daunting aspect of the entire selection process, but me? I had absolutely nothing to lose. I couldn't see myself being picked, so I really was just glad to have made it this far. They asked the questions, and I answered to the best of my ability and tried to be myself.

Others seemed to go out of their way to impress the decision makers, or, to put it a little less delicately, to suck up. They would brag about having drinks with this person or that, certain that it was going to make a difference. Guys like John Young and George Abbey, then the head of flight crew operations, kept showing up, and folks would gravitate toward them as if they maybe had the astronaut assignments right there in their back pockets.

If somebody took the time to shake my hand and talk to me, I spoke to them without ever considering if they might be able to help me become an astronaut. Cynics might suggest that my seeming indifference was a ploy in and of itself, but it was not. The fact is, the longer things played out that week in Houston, the more I became convinced that flying on board the space shuttle was not going to happen for me.

Others knew the right people, and, quite simply, I did not. Again, I was left with a sense of peace in my spirit that I had done the very best that I could. I had not tried to be someone I wasn't, and while my time at NASA had been a good experience, I was not going to apply again.

Marine Corps Air Station El Toro, not far from Los Angeles, had been the home of Marine aviation on the West Coast since World War II. Instead of returning to Japan, I was transferred there following my adventure in Texas. About a month after I arrived, I got a phone call in my office.

On the other end of the line was George Abbey, whose presence during the selection process had been so noticeable. His question was simple and to the point.

Are you still interested in coming to Houston?

Chapter 7

David Hilmers, NASA Astronaut

Just like that, I was officially an astronaut candidate—or ASCAN, for short—one of nineteen who were selected in 1980. For some of my classmates, the call from Houston and George Abbey was the culmination of a lifelong dream. There were many stories about how people reacted, from whoops and yells to outright tears.

Me, I was much more nonchalant about my new job, if for no other reason than I had so thoroughly convinced myself that it wasn't going to happen. I had been laying the groundwork to continue my pursuit of getting into medical school, so joining NASA meant that I had to once again switch gears. There wasn't a chance in the world that I might turn it down, but there were definitely things I would have to consider.

What would becoming an astronaut mean in the grand scheme of my career path? What would it mean to my family? There were a million details to be ironed out before it would ever sink in that I was about to begin training to fly in space.

If it all seemed like a dream, NASA issued a press release on May 29, 1980, confirming that I had, in fact, been selected along with eight pilots and ten other mission specialists. Until I actually saw it in print, I was somewhat suspicious that I had been the victim of a prank phone call! So there it was, in black and white, with the old NASA worm logo—so called because of its stylized script—right there at the top of the page. A few weeks later came another release confirming that we would be reporting to Houston on July 7 to begin a year of training. At the bottom of the page was a note to news editors that the astronaut candidates would be made available for interviews.

Wait a second. Interviews? Like, with reporters? Why in the world would anybody be interested in anything I had to say? I hadn't flown in space yet. I was just a guy who happened to be in the right place at the right time when NASA called. That kind of stuff was reserved for famous astronauts like Neil Armstrong, John Glenn, and John Young, wasn't it? It had never dawned on me that part of my new job requirement was to sit down with reporters scribbling notes for stories they were going to write and pointing television cameras my way.

Nevertheless, I was surprised by how comfortable I felt during my earliest days at NASA. The astronaut office was still mostly active duty and former military officers and was run like a civilian version of a military aircraft squadron, and I was definitely used to that!

The men and women who accompanied me into the astronaut office that year would go on to become some of the heaviest hitters of the shuttle era.

Charlie Bolden, who also served in the Marines before his NASA days, served as pilot on two space shuttle missions and commanded two others. In 2009, he was appointed by President Barrack Obama as NASA administrator—the highest position in the agency. Five of the eight pilot astronauts in our class led shuttle crews, and one, Mike Smith, lost his life in the *Challenger* accident before getting his shot at command.

The mission specialists were no slouches, either. Two, Bill Fisher and Jim Bagian, were already the medical doctors that I still very much wanted to be. Jerry Ross wound up with seven flights to his credit, giving him the record for the most trips to space in the annals of human spaceflight. Jerry dove headlong into the training pool for spacewalks, and eventually became *the* go-to guy on all things having to do with EVA—extravehicular activity, a NASA-speak term for spacewalking. He spent countless hours in the Neutral Buoyancy Laboratory—another NASA-ese phrase to describe the humongous pool in which astronauts trained for EVAs. That was despite the fact that Jerry couldn't swim very well when he became an astronaut. Not long after Jerry made his last flight, fellow 1980 classmate Franklin Chang-Diaz joined him in the history books with *his* seventh journey to orbit. In all, the 1980 class of astronauts took part in sixty-two space shuttle flights—including *Challenger*'s ill-fated final voyage.

Franklin and I became close, due at least in part to our common lifestyle. What's the best way to put this? We both liked to live as inexpensively as possible, and when Franklin arrived in Houston, you could literally put your foot through the floorboard of the car he was driving. Don't laugh—to this day, I still putter around in a Toyota Tercel that's nearly twenty years old. When he first moved to Texas, Franklin lived in an old farmhouse. That prompted us to dig up the yard and plant a garden. We weren't very good at it, but we did manage to enjoy a few vegetables. Throughout his years at NASA, Franklin worked on a plasma rocket that may change the way we explore our corner of the universe.

All in all, the 1980 astronaut candidate group was a laid-back group. We took our classes and went on our trips to most of the NASA centers around the country during our yearlong apprenticeship. On one visit, we went out to New Mexico and Colorado to study the area's geology. Why? The space shuttle wasn't going to land anywhere except right back on Earth, so the application wasn't exactly clear to us at the time. It was only later that we found the information very useful for Earth observations from space. We enjoyed the adventure, figured that it was a nice getaway trip, and if looking at a bunch of rocks was the price we had to pay, then so be it.

―✦―

STS-1 launched on April 12, 1981, carrying John Young and Bob Crippen to orbit on the very first shakedown flight of the space shuttle. While my classmates and I weren't officially considered astronauts yet, we were already beginning to wonder when our own turns to fly might come.

Ever since Americans began strapping into the pointy ends of rockets, being assigned to a spaceflight had been somewhat of a mystery. Ability was obviously an important ingredient, but it wasn't the *only* factor. For the duration of my stay at NASA, I was as apolitical as it was possible to be. Others could try to claw their way up the ladder, but that simply was not my personality. I was clueless about any maneuvering that was taking place behind the scenes, and anything that I did happen to hear was third- or fourth-hand.

Dave Leestma was the first of our class to be assigned to a flight, and there were a few who took the announcement with an almost bitter disappointment. Me? I felt incredibly blessed just to be in the astronaut office—how could I possibly quibble over when I got selected to a crew?

Dave was a really talented individual, and I thought that he was very deserving to be the first from our group to fly. That's not to say that I wasn't looking forward to my own assignment, because that most definitely wasn't the case. I would show up to a public appearance and try to explain that while I was an astronaut, I hadn't yet flown. Folks would show up expecting to meet a famous space shuttle astronaut like Sally Ride, the first American woman in space, but instead, they got me. The slide shows that I presented were always from somebody else's flight—I wanted to show off photographs from my own mission!

Chapter 8

Blastoff!

As much as I had been anticipating my first crew assignment, when it finally did happen in November 1983, I was hit with a whole slew of mixed emotions.

I was on something called the "launch-ready standby crew" for a possible Department of Defense (DoD) flight. Even those of us on the crew didn't know what that meant. It didn't have an official flight number, and it hadn't been assigned to any of the three orbiters that were in the fleet at the time — *Columbia*, which made the first flight in 1981; *Discovery*; and *Challenger*. The rest of the crew included commander Bo Bobko, pilot Ron Grabe, and fellow mission specialists Bob Stewart and Mike Mullane.

For months, the five of us trained for tasks that might or might not actually take place. We did our jobs and did them well, but it was sometimes disconcerting not to know for sure when or even if we would fly. It wasn't until February 15, 1985, that the DoD voyage of STS-51J was officially announced, with Mike being moved onto another crew and replaced a few weeks later by payload specialist Bill Pailes.

Bill was a part of the Air Force's Manned Spaceflight Engineer Program, which trained military personnel to deploy top-secret payloads from the shuttle's cargo bay. The primary objectives of the space shuttle's DoD flights were so closely guarded that press kits weren't distributed and public countdowns didn't begin until just minutes before launch. It must have driven reporters crazy when they couldn't listen in on our air-to-ground communications as they usually did, but that didn't stop them from all kinds of speculation on what we would be doing "up there." I couldn't shout from the rooftops about the mission, but as a longtime member of the military, I knew exactly why that was the case.

The long and short of it was that I was on a crew, and we finally had an official flight number. Originally scheduled to launch in September 1985, STS-51J would be taking the brand-new space shuttle *Atlantis* out for a spin on her first trip to orbit.

—◄ ▬ ►—

The five of us were fairly quiet guys who didn't make a lot of noise, Bo included. We didn't raise much of a ruckus over anything, and as a result, we all got along really well. All of us came from military backgrounds—Bo, Ron, and Bill were Air Force, while Bob was Army.

We all gave each other a little bit of good-natured inter-service ribbing, like the time I reminded Bob how tough it was that he had to attend Army basic training down at the Holiday Inn Express.

Of the four crews on which I served, STS-51J was probably the most uniformly religious. A group of us in the astronaut office routinely held Bible studies throughout my time with the agency, and on this flight in particular, we all seemed to be on the same basic page when it came to our faith. So it meant the world to me that we said a prayer together on our way out to the launch pad on October 3, 1985.

I had a great seat for the launch, up on the flight deck, right behind Ron in the pilot's seat. We wore what amounted to coveralls, motorcycle helmets, and small survival vests in the days before the *Challenger* accident, making it fairly easy to move around. After lying on my back for what seemed like forever, I unfastened my safety harnesses and wiggled around to sit on the back of my seat. Bob, situated to my immediate left, did the same. That's the way we stayed until we got to the standard hold at T-minus nine minutes. At that point, we settled back into our seats and secured our belts as the seconds continued to melt away.

And then, boom! We were on our way.

Although I never had much of a problem with a condition very delicately known as "space motion sickness," being in weightlessness did take some getting used to.

I wasn't queasy, but I wasn't ready for a huge meal the first day or so, either. Better to be safe than sorry! There were a few other little nagging things, like having trouble getting to sleep, as well as a headache and backache.

Other than that, however, zero g was one of the greatest experiences anyone could ever imagine. There was no dropping anything. If you let something go very carefully, it would just stay there, suspended in midair right in front of your face. That made eating especially fun, although we often had to grab grub on the quick due to our busy schedules. For just over four days, that's how we lived and worked in space.

Believe me, I would love to describe exactly what it was that I did on orbit in the fall of 1985. But since it was a secret DoD mission devoted to protecting the security of our country, I can't. Just know that I was very proud to serve. Just like that, it seemed, the flight was over and we were landing at Edwards Air Force Base in California.

—◄┃►—

As strange as it may seem, by the time *Atlantis*'s wheels came to a stop, I was already back in line for another flight. The *Centaur* rocket was a beast in every sense of the word, and it was the job of the STS-61F crew to figure out a way to work with it.

Thin-skinned and pressure-stabilized, plans called for the rocket to boost the *Ulysses* interplanetary probe to study the polar regions of the sun. It was to be fueled by a mixture of liquid oxygen and liquid hydrogen, and while that may not sound threatening, it would have been very much like launching with what was basically a bomb located in the cargo bay. That was risky enough, but to get the monstrosity to orbit, the three main engines would have to be pushed all the way up to 109 percent of their rated thrust. Then, if some sort of early emergency forced a launch abort, the *Centaur*'s fuel would have to be vented while returning back to KSC.

John Young called it the "Death Star" mission, and Rick Hauck, who'd been named commander of STS-61F, actually offered us the chance to leave the crew gracefully due to the dangers involved. Looking back, it's hard to imagine that we had the audacity to even attempt such a risky flight. NASA was about to learn a very, very hard lesson in what that could ultimately mean.

Chapter 9

Challenger

Those of us in the meeting room stared at the television monitor, not believing what we were seeing.

Moments after the launch of STS-51L on January 28, 1986, *Challenger* was destroyed in a gigantic ball of flame and smoke. We gasped, knowing that the crew—commander Dick Scobee; pilot Mike Smith; mission specialists Ellison Onizuka, Judy Resnik, and Ron McNair; payload specialist Greg Jarvis; and teacher in space Christa McAuliffe—could not survive the terrible inferno.

They were our friends and coworkers, and in an instant, all of them were gone. Shock resonated through the room, accompanied by almost complete silence as the room emptied. There was no reason to meet anymore because the space shuttle was not going to fly anytime soon.

Once I made it home that night—it was my birthday—I sat down at our piano and played Canon in G by the German baroque composer Johann Pachelbel over and over again for hours on end. The melancholy music washed over the room, its notes speaking to the sadness welling deep down inside me. Life would never be the same for any of us at NASA.

Mike, in particular, was a really good friend of mine. Members of the same astronaut class, we had a shared interest in learning how the stock market worked. As we flew together to one place or another, we compared notes on buying stocks, which ones were doing well and which ones weren't. A native of Beaufort, North Carolina, Mike was an incredibly competent and solid guy to whom people could relate on any number of levels. After I bought his used lawn mower, Mike good-naturedly gave me a hard time about being cheap. The joke was on him, though, because I used that used lawn mower for more than fifteen years.

I knew the rest of the crew less well, but their loss still stung very deeply. Judy was funny and down-to-earth, and she wouldn't hesitate to put you in your place with a zinger if she felt you needed it. Better yet, she could take a joke as well.

The grief we all felt was on a couple of different levels, the first of which was deeply personal. All of us from the top of the agency on down agonized over what the families of the *Challenger* crew were going through. What should we do to help? Could we do more? The flip side of grief was for the NASA family in general. All of us

Smoke billowing from the *Challenger* explosion.

had a vested interest in the shuttle program, but nobody seemed to know what the future held. Would the shuttle ever even fly again? Personally and professionally, uncertainty lurked around every corner.

—◁▷—

As the weeks passed and the initial shock began to wear off, President Ronald Reagan ordered a commission to investigate the causes of the accident. Chaired by former United States Attorney General and Secretary of State William P. Rogers, the panel also included Neil Armstrong, Sally Ride, and Chuck Yeager.

That summer, the committee's report found that the subfreezing temperatures on the morning of the launch had caused an O-ring seal on the right solid rocket booster to fail. Flames spewed out of the failed seal, burning a hole in the familiar orange external tank as *Challenger* and her crew ascended. Seventy-three seconds into the flight, the tank exploded and the vehicle simply couldn't keep up with the aerodynamic forces that were tearing it apart.

The accident itself was bad enough, but another critical issue was laid bare. There had been warnings against launch because of the freezing temperatures—there were huge icicles hanging off the gantry at the launch pad, for crying out loud! Those concerns were either shouted down or ignored altogether, just as they had been with my scheduled STS-61F mission. Meeting a schedule that was throwing more and more flights into the mix every year got to be too much, and we paid for it with the loss of a space shuttle and seven wonderful people.

Moving on meant starting from scratch and reexamining everything we possibly could in order to determine where improvements could be made. STS-61F had been canceled, but for the shuttle to ever fly again safely, we had to comb through hardware, software, systems, mission rules, and our culture as a whole. Never before had NASA lost a crew during flight, and the fact that it had come so perilously close during *Gemini 8* and *Apollo 13* had basically sealed its reputation for being able to handle any emergency. There's nothing wrong with those kinds of heroics, of course, but it's also very easy to get

The crew of the *Challenger*.

complacent. The myth very sadly ended when *Challenger* fell from the sky.

We were good at NASA, but we weren't so good that we couldn't make serious mistakes. We could, and we did. The question now was whether or not we could learn from what had gone wrong.

The space shuttle was going to return to orbit, but not until NASA was comfortable in doing so. Deciding to fly was always going to be a hard decision, based solely on the number of factors that had to be taken into consideration. But in the aftermath of the accident, safety became much more of a concern. In my parents' generation, a Japanese attack on the Hawaiian Islands caused the world to "Remember Pearl Harbor!" After the loss of my friends, the need for constant vigilance was clear.

Courtesy of NASA

The hearses line up at the memorial for the *Challenger* crew.

Remember *Challenger!*
Remember *Challenger* and be safe!
Remember *Challenger* and never let anything like that happen again!
Remember *Challenger!*

Chapter 10

Return to Flight

As soon as it became clear that there was going to be another shuttle on the launch pad, the whispers began. Who was going to be on it when it flew?

I had been in line to fly on 61F before the accident but really had no idea what that meant now. If Rick Hauck was chosen to lead the first post-*Challenger* flight, I figured there would be a fairly decent chance that I would be right there alongside him. The decision was out of my hands, so I didn't worry about it and left the political posturing to others. It wasn't until we were called to George Abbey's office that I knew for sure that I would be on the Return to Flight mission of STS-26.

Three of us from the canceled STS-61F team remained on STS-26: Rick as commander, along with myself and Mike Lounge as mission specialists. STS-61F pilot Roy Bridges left NASA to command a test-flight wing at

Edwards Air Force Base, so he was replaced as the "right seater" by Dick Covey. One more spot on the crew went to George "Pinky" Nelson, who had been on the last successful flight before the *Challenger* accident. The official announcement was made on January 9, 1987, nearly twenty-one months before we actually launched.

Remember how I could say virtually nothing about my first space shuttle flight, STS-51J, because it was a top-secret Department of Defense mission? It's almost humorous to think about the differences between that flight and my second, because of the glare of the spotlight that was on STS-26 almost from the time we were selected as its crew. The attention had always come with the territory, but the cameras and the reporters and the questions about what was on our minds as we prepared to fly after *Challenger* sometimes got intrusive. One television crew filmed a long training session, and in the cramped confines of the simulator, its presence was, to be blunt, a bit obtrusive.

The fact that we had the attention of the media was not lost on the rest of our comrades in the astronaut office, and don't think for a second that they didn't give us a hard time about it. Poor Rick and Dick. They attended one function in downtown Houston where they were introduced complete with spotlights, music, and smoke machines. The crew of STS-27, the next flight after ours and a DoD flight to boot, re-created the scene during the weekly astronaut office meeting the following Monday.

Much to their delight and Rick's and Dick's chagrin, fire extinguishers were set off for the smoke effect and

Courtesy of NASA

The midnight rollout with all the lights!

somebody cued up "I'm Proud To Be an American" on a cassette player (the song that had been played earlier at the downtown reception). Mike, Pinky, and I thought it was funny, because, after all, we hadn't been at the soiree in Houston and therefore weren't in the crosshairs of the joke.

There were a few opportunities that I truly enjoyed, and none more than the July 4, 1988, midnight rollout of *Discovery* from the Vehicle Assembly Building at the Kennedy Space Center to the launch pad. Everybody else on the crew was tied up, so I had the privilege of speaking at the ceremony. Bathed in lights, the vehicle was awe-inspiring and beautiful. The setting was all teed up, so I just had to hit the shot with a few appropriate remarks. It wound up being one of the better speeches I've ever made, if I do say so myself! Bob Crippen, the former shuttle commander who spoke before me, grinned later and asked, "Where did that come from?" Once Rick Hauck saw a video of the event, his response was even better.

You sounded like Thomas Jefferson.

Maybe not, but what I did feel was an overwhelming feeling of pride to represent America on this crew. That's what I wanted to get across, nothing more, nothing less.

—◄ ▮ ►—

In a very real sense, the looming launch of STS-26 became a metaphor for life.

Because there's usually no way of knowing when we might face death, many choose to put off or even ignore the opportunity to walk with Christ. I knew that the day I launched on *Discovery* could very well be the last day of my life, but rather than dreading that fact, it helped me become a better person. I've tried to live the rest of my life that way, knowing that I will soon be coming face-to-face with Jesus. I have failed in that quest more times than I would care to consider, but it's still a daily goal.

My priorities were in order during the months leading up to the launch. I was more aware of the people around me and their needs, and tried to help out whenever and wherever I could. My wife and kids were obviously concerned about the flight, but they were great about not letting it show. I often sat down with twelve-year-old Matt and nine-year-old Dan to discuss the dangers associated with the flight of STS-26, and as a family, we prayed and read Scripture.

Later, a newspaper reporter asked Dan who his hero was, and his reply caught me off guard.

My dad, because he sits down and talks with me.

It was one of the nicest things any of my family has ever said about me. It was how I wanted to be remembered in case I didn't make it back.

I prepared for the impending launch in other ways as well. At the small local church where I was an elder and piano player, I gave the Sunday morning children's sermon several weeks before the launch and just before we went into quarantine. I used a visual example of filling a pail with large and small objects to illustrate how things will fit together when we choose to honor God first. It was a very emotional experience for me.

One of the kindest expressions of support for the NASA team came when President Reagan made a special visit to Houston just to speak to the workers at JSC. After his speech, he met with the crew and our families. I will never forget how warmly he spoke to each of us and how genuinely he expressed his wishes for our safety on the mission. We met with him in a big hangar and a large limousine drove in to pick him up when the time came. What was touching was that he stopped the car twice as he was leaving and waved two more times to us. While it was gratifying, I could not help but wonder whether he felt that he was never going to see us again!

—◂▸—

When the crew of STS-26 got to the launch pad on the morning of September 29, 1988, we knew full well that NASA's future was riding on the mission. It's not a stretch to say that another accident probably would have meant the end of America's human spaceflight program for a very long time. For the first time, we were wearing the now-familiar pumpkin-colored "launch and entry suits." These suits were designed to provide protection from a *Challenger*-type decompression accident, offering the hope that we could bail out and survive. While the suits were hot and bulky and made the wait on the launch pad much more uncomfortable, we were glad that at least the possibility existed to escape another accident.

When the countdown clock finally reached zero, it had been nearly three years since the *Challenger* accident. It was impossible not to think of the crew of STS-51L, especially after an alarm rang seconds after we lifted off. It turned out to be a relatively minor issue, but you better believe it got my attention, since I was seated right behind the center console on the flight deck. It took eight and a half minutes to make it to orbit, at which point the shuttle's three main engines cut off—known in NASA-speak as MECO. Mike would later call them the longest eight and a half minutes of his life. Once we were parked safely on orbit, I made a formal request in my best military tone.

Commander, request permission to celebrate.

Rick's reply came in the very same starched, military manner.

Permission granted.

For the next ten seconds or so, we all let out a few whoops and hollers. We had made it!

Cynics who criticized the relatively sparse flight plan were probably missing the point. Returning to flight meant that if we could launch and land safely, the mission would have been a success. If we had not made it back home safe and sound, it wouldn't have mattered how many activities had been packed into the flight plan. Here's the thing—we weren't up there twiddling our thumbs with no reason to be there. There were plenty of experiments to conduct, and a little more than six hours into the four-day flight, we deployed a Tracking and Data Relay Satellite designed to improve communications between the ground and orbiting spacecraft.

We also couldn't let the flight pass without honoring those we'd lost on *Challenger*, and so I sat down and tried to plan out what each of the five of us would say. I wanted people to be aware of their sacrifice, but also to tell the world why it was important for us to continue flying in space. As we read the homage, various views of Earth were beamed down to give those watching an idea of the majestic splendor visible from the shuttle's flight deck.

Courtesy of NASA

The crew honoring the members of the *Challenger*. Note the photo in the background.

I began the short memorial service by reading from one of the small cue cards that I had made for each of the crew. "We'd like to take just a few moments today to share with you some of the sights that we've been so privileged to view over the past several days," I read. "As we watch along with you, many emotions well up in our hearts—joy, for America's return to space; gratitude, for our nation's support through difficult times; thanksgiving, for the safety of our crew; reverence, for those whose sacrifice made our journey possible."

Next came Mike, then Dick, Pinky, and, last but not least, our skipper, Rick. We would never forget the crew that came right before us. Never.

Sporting our Hawaiian shirts.

We had a very brief chance late in the flight to let our hair down, so to speak. Gearing up for STS-26 had been an emotional journey, and the staff at NASA's tracking station in Hawaii had sent us a set of shirts to boost our spirits.

These weren't any ordinary shirts. They were colorful Hawaiian shirts, the kind workers in the Orbiter Processing Facility liked to wear on their "loud and proud" Fridays when casual attire was allowed. We took them along on the flight and put them on for a few minutes of fun. I went for a swim through the mid-deck after Dick "surfed" on Pinky's back. The video gets the crowd going every time I show it now, more than a quarter of a century later! Dick's "loud and proud" shirt is currently on display at the Johnson Space Center visitors'

Courtesy of NASA

Greeting Vice President Bush after successfully completing our mission.

center, while mine is ... is ... well ... it's around here somewhere!

After the cameras clicked off, we stowed everything, set the seats up, and got back into our launch and reentry pressure suits. Rick brought us down at Edwards Air Force Base just past 9:37 a.m. local time, the mission complete. Vice President George H. W. Bush was there to greet us as we left the crew cabin. America was finally back in space!

Chapter 11

The Best Flight Ever (Maybe)

Rob Kelso—one of the flight directors for my next flight, STS-36—once told a reporter that the mission was, in his view, one of the two or three greatest in the entire thirty-year history of the space shuttle program. He couldn't elaborate, however, because it was another classified, top-secret venture dedicated to support the Department of Defense. It was an amazing flight, Rob concluded, that virtually no one would ever know about.

Was STS-36, which launched in the early morning hours of February 28, 1990, an important mission that helped keep America and its interests secure? It most definitely was. That was enough for me, regardless of whether the public ever actually knows about its accomplishments. After the experience of my last mission, it was nice to be on a flight that faced little or no attention from the media and the public at large.

Whatever happened or didn't happen during STS-36, it was something of an adventure even getting to the launch pad. And somewhere along the way, an old dream of mine was reawakened.

—◄ ▮ ►—

STS-36 was commanded by John Creighton, with John Casper serving as the pilot. Mike Mullane, Pierre Thuot, and I were the mission specialists. Like every crew before us and every one to follow, we found ourselves quarantined in Houston and then in Florida after making the trip to KSC for the launch. The accommodations are comfortable enough, but it's not home and the people you're with are not your family. The purpose of quarantine was to prevent any of the astronauts and their closest support personnel from catching any last-minute bugs, but at least in our case, it didn't work.

An initial launch attempt on February 22, 1990, was scrubbed when John Creighton developed an upper respiratory infection. He wasn't the only one not feeling well. A tainted water supply gave not only John Casper and me staph infections, but other support personnel as well. To make matters worse, our sleep cycles were being shifted because we were going to be launching in the middle of the night. That meant that our body clocks were thrown out of whack by sleeping during the daytime hours and staying up through the night.

While I was trying to doze one afternoon, someone in the next room kept me awake while vomiting. Trust me, it's not easy to sleep when you're visualizing that whatever the person next door has will catch up with you when you are on orbit!

Another scrub followed two days later due to expected bad weather. We made it out to the launch pad on February 25 and 26, but again faced delays, one because of an issue with a range safety computer and the other, again, for weather. Were we ever going to get this show on the road? The decision was made to send us back to Houston for a day or two to do some simulator runs before the next launch attempt.

The delays grew tiresome for the kids, and my son Matt wanted to get back to school. Don Puddy, who had replaced George Abbey as the director of NASA's flight crew operations division, went out of his way to make sure that Matt was able to fly back with us to Houston on one of the transport aircraft. Don earned a special place in my heart for that act of kindness, which was actually outside the usual rules for family members.

The illnesses, sleep shifts, and delays had already made for a difficult launch experience by the time we headed back out to the pad for the third time. With nothing to do but lie there and listen to Mike Mullane's jokes during the long two-and-a-half-hour launch window, I had to find something to distract myself.

John Casper, the rookie pilot on our flight, was seated to my right front and directly ahead of Pierre Thuot on the flight deck. The wind would sometimes catch *Atlantis*, the external tank, and the solid rocket boosters just right and sway the whole stack back and forth ever so slightly. It could be a little unsettling if you weren't

Courtesy of NASA

The cockpit.

prepared for it, so Pierre and I decided then and there we were going to help the situation along a little bit. The wind blew, the stack moved ... and we grabbed the back of John's seat and gave it a good shake. His helmet limited his peripheral vision, so John couldn't see what we were up to just behind him. The wind blew again and this time we shook his seat even more. Let's just say that John's eyes got really big until he discovered what we were up to!

Finally, at just past 2:50 a.m. local time, we left the pad in the most awesome light display I had ever encountered—and I was right in the middle of it. In the darkness of the early morning hours, the fire and flashes out in front of us were lighting up the sky. Because of our record launch inclination of sixty-two degrees from the

Earth's equator, our path actually took the light show north up the East Coast and over land at some points.

Sometimes on orbit, it seemed like we were literally flying through green and blue plumes of the aurora borealis (the northern lights), which we would see at the most northerly latitudes. Our low altitude gave us the best views of Earth I would ever have while in space. The details you could pick up were simply amazing. When it came down to it, the mission really was one of the greatest NASA had ever flown.

Or not. I can't say!

Chapter 12

Medical School, Anyone?

Earth wasn't the only thing that had come into better focus for me in the months following STS-36.

A few months after I returned from the flight, I was assigned to be a backup crew member for an upcoming mission with a very short launch window. If one of the mission specialists on that crew became ill or unable to fly, they would need to have someone step in on very short notice. As part of the training for that flight, I was doing an ascent simulation. Our simulation team was almost like family to us, and any problems they threw at us were in the spirit of making us as good a crew as we could be for the mission. They felt that by being tough on us, they were helping to ensure that we could handle any emergency.

This run was no different. They threw what seemed like every conceivable glitch and breakdown at us ...

and I had already seen them all before. I knew what was coming. The patterns were the same, almost like every move was being telegraphed beforehand. As I walked out of the simulator that day, the nagging feeling returned that this was not my life's calling.

Did I want to be someone who knew the right switch to flip on the space shuttle, or was it time to move on? Sure, there were a lot of things that I had not had the opportunity to do as an astronaut—a spacewalk, for example. Was I willing to wait years for something that may never materialize? Then and there, the childhood dream of one day becoming a doctor resurfaced just like it had so many other times. This time, however, it wasn't going to go away. It was time to either put up, or shut up and quit thinking about it ever again. How could I possibly allow myself to keep going back to that dream, only to do nothing about it? Sure, there was a very real chance that I would fail.

But I had to give it a shot. The feeling that I could help the less fortunate in some small way as a physician prodded me forward.

Whenever I talked to my good friends and fellow astronauts Norm Thagard and Ellen Baker, who just so happened to be physicians themselves, they always encouraged me to go for it. So in the summer of 1990, I enrolled in an advanced life support course to make sure this was truly something I was meant to pursue. It took just a class or two for it to become clear that I didn't just like the work after all. I *loved* it, and from there on out,

I lit the afterburners in an all-out assault on getting into medical school once and for all.

I was offered a fourth spaceflight as the payload commander for a mission that was a couple of years down the road. Four years hence I could maybe have another flight under my belt, or I could have an MD degree. To me, the choice was obvious; I turned the flight down.

The first hurdle I needed to clear was to get past the Medical College Admission Test (MCAT). I had it all figured out. I was going to take the MCAT in the spring of 1991 and then apply to medical schools that fall. And, at long last, I would actually begin attending med school in the late summer of 1992 if all went according to plan. With that schedule, I could retire from the Marines with a full twenty years of service, and I would be able to go to school with a monthly retirement check and the GI Bill to pay the tuition. Sure, it was going to be a very, very aggressive timeline, but I had faced such things before and come through in good shape.

I enrolled in organic chemistry and biology courses at a local community college in Houston—classes I wasn't even going to be able to finish before taking the MCAT—and the radio was on in my car as I headed to school for the first night of class. What I heard got my attention. The date was January 17, 1991—the night coalition forces led by the United States began a massive aerial bombardment of Iraq in what was known as Operation Desert Storm.

I was torn for a couple of reasons, and the first of those was that I was literally leaving NASA in my rearview

Medical School, Anyone?

Courtesy of NASA

Pool training at NASA.

mirror as I drove the fifteen miles or so to school. On top of that, I was sure I had friends in harm's way in the skies over Baghdad while I was off trying to start a whole new career. Praying for their safety and well-being, I sat down in that classroom and tried my best to concentrate.

The next three months were a blur. I took the classes and then crammed on my own to get far enough ahead on what I needed to know for the MCAT. I would get up at 5:00 a.m. and study for a couple of hours before leaving for work at NASA, then pick right back up where I left off afterward. I practiced writing for the essay portion of the test, because I figured that I needed to do really well there in order to make up for any shortcomings on the parts of the test covered by the classes I had not even taken. With just a couple of weeks to go before the big test, one of the most important I would ever take in my life, I was putting in as much work as I possibly could to prepare myself for it.

It was a done deal. A new chapter in my life was just beginning. I was never going to fly in space again.

And then Sonny Carter died.

Chapter 13

The Unexpected Flight

Astronaut Sonny Carter was universally loved, but, wow, he was as competitive as the day is long.

Sonny was an Eagle Scout and played soccer, ran track, and became an intramural wrestling champion during his college days at Emory University. That was impressive enough, but the native of Macon, Georgia, later played professional soccer with the Atlanta Chiefs of the North American Soccer League while in medical school. I was later to learn how incredible it was that he could both go to medical school and play professional soccer. He went on to fly the F–4 Phantom in the Navy, and wound up attending both the famous Navy Fighter Weapons School and Naval Test Pilot School. Physician. College athlete. Professional soccer player. Top gun. Test pilot. You name it, and Sonny was all about becoming the best of the best.

Even when we went running together, it was never just a leisurely jog. It always—*always*—ended up becoming a race to the finish, and I remember in particular a couple of epic runs that we had along the banks of the Potomac River when we happened to be in Washington D.C. together. His driven nature extended to my own plans to attend medical school. He encouraged me to follow in his footsteps, but in a unique I-dare-you-to-try-it kind of way.

Sonny was on his way from Houston to speak at a Rotary Club convention when his commercial airplane crashed in Brunswick, Georgia, on April 5, 1991. All twenty-three people on board the flight—including Sonny and former United States Senator John Tower—were killed. A veteran of one shuttle flight already, he had been assigned as a mission specialist on STS-42 when his plane went down in southern Georgia.

Ron Grabe and I were members of the same astronaut candidate class, and we made our first spaceflights together on STS-51J. The flight of STS-42 was to be Ron's first as a commander. One of my closest friends in the office was Norm Thagard, and he was the "payload commander," the astronaut in charge of the experiments on board. I was so busy studying for the MCAT that I'm not quite sure how it all worked out, but the two of them evidently made it known that they wanted me to take Sonny's place. Dan Brandenstein, then the chief of the astronaut office, came to me with the idea.

The suggestion took me by surprise, and my first re-action was to protest and try to remind Dan of my plans for medical school. But because Ron and Norm had gone to bat for me, I prayed about it and made a decision. I would do both. I would train for the flight and continue preparing for medical school. No problem, right?

Dan agreed and, gracious as always, offered to work with me as much as possible on scheduling and so forth. Within just a couple of days, I started training as a mission specialist on STS-42, which was slated to launch in January 1992 and was designated as International Microgravity Laboratory 1. It carried the Spacelab in the cargo bay, which allowed us to work on a wide range of scientific experiments, including life sciences, botany, physics, and materials processing. For the first time, I was to be mostly a scientist on this mission. I had a ton of studying ahead of me, not only for the MCAT, but for the mission itself.

I took the MCAT as planned, and when my scores came back, I was pleased with the results. The science results were better than I had dared expect, and while my overall score wasn't exactly going to blow anybody away, it was certainly respectable. In the summer, I applied for early admission at the Baylor College of Medicine in Houston and was accepted! I'd done it! I had to chuckle a bit about the letter that I had received from Baylor about my age some fifteen years before.

As long as I had dreamed of this very moment, however, there was no time to celebrate. As I continued with the premed classes I was taking, I was also now in full-bore training for a space shuttle mission. Sometimes I would leave training a couple of hours early so I could make a night class. Other times I flew back and forth between Houston and Huntsville, Alabama, where some of the experiment training for the flight was being conducted and where we trained on the Spacelab mock-up.

We even spent some time in the Netherlands, training on some of the European Space Agency experiments that we were flying. I was studying as hard as I could, not only for school, but also for the scientific research that was to be conducted on the flight. But things, as they have a way of doing, worked out. My last final exam for my premed courses was in December 1991, about a month before we were due to launch.

The crew of STS-42, which also included pilot Steve Oswald, mission specialist Bill Readdy, and payload specialists Roberta Bondar and Ulf Merbold, was slated for around-the-clock research during the flight on two separate work shifts. Again I'd tried to alter my sleep cycle, but this time, it didn't work for me.

By the time we hit the launch pad, the crew members on my shift had already been up for eight or nine hours. I was exhausted, but while the plan was for my team to sleep soon after ascent, I would defy *anybody* to go through the launch of a space shuttle and then almost immediately try to go to sleep. It just didn't work like that!

One of my first tasks on the flight was to be strapped into a chair that could be rotated at various speeds while on its back, sitting sideways, or sitting straight up. While doing so, we also had to wear a helmet that could mea-

Courtesy of NASA

Crew of the STS-42.

sure our eye movements and visors that fit over each eye to provide visual stimuli. Part of the difficulty with this experiment was trying to keep your eyes open so that the experimenters could record the eye movements; the other problem was that I was asked to do it on flight day 1, which is when astronauts are most prone to space motion sickness. Any head movement tends to make it worse.

That wasn't my major hurdle, though. We did this experiment almost every day during the mission and I found it very easy to doze off. Just imagine being tired and put into a dark place. Even with the rotations, it was easy to go to sleep, despite the efforts of the ground team (who could see my eyes from the cameras inside the helmet I was wearing) and the encouragement from Ulf Merbold, who was my experienced and brilliant partner during the mission. Going to sleep whenever there was an opportunity was a skill that I perfected during my later years in medical school and residency and have never lost. Sometimes I would sing aloud to keep awake, even the Marine Corps hymn at times!

On my first three flights, the crews had been confined to the relatively small area of the flight deck and mid-deck. But with the Spacelab tucked into *Discovery*'s payload on STS-42, there seemed to be all kinds of room, almost like a space station. It was really fun to push off from the mid-deck, go through the tunnel air lock, and then float all the way through the Spacelab. But because the flight plan was so packed with experiments, there was little time for such fun.

Or reflection.

It wasn't until we were getting ready to return to Earth that it finally sank in that I was never going to pass this way again. I was never going to be in crew quarters again. I was never going to ride the Astrovan to the launch pad again or be strapped in for launch. I was never going to experience weightlessness again. When Ron brought *Discovery* to a stop at Edwards Air Force Base on January 30, 1992, my spaceflight career was over.

Over four flights, I had spent more than 493 hours in space. I'd made 329 laps around the globe while on orbit, and traveled 8,121,753 miles. Those accomplish-

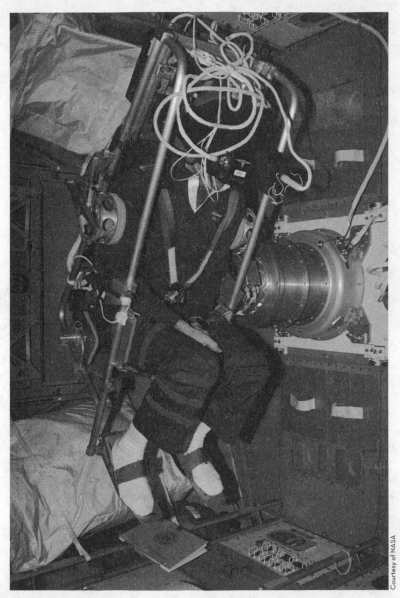

The rotating chair.

The landing of *Discovery*.

ments meant a lot to me, but I couldn't help but be excited about what the future held for me as a physician. I was ready.

Or was I?

Chapter 14

Second Thoughts and a Great Rebound

Colonel David C. Hilmers, United States Marine Corps.

That has a nice ring to it, doesn't it? I had been promoted a few months before my final shuttle flight, but in order to retire at that pay grade and receive a bigger retirement check, I had to continue in the military for another year.

I briefly thought about delaying my entry into medical school for a year, but I decided that now was the time to start. However, I thought that I might be able to stay on a few extra months and make some extra money as I began medical school at Baylor. I was the ultimate multitasker, and this was going to prove it. There was only one problem. The plan very nearly backfired on me.

Classes at Baylor began in July 1992, and on the weekends, I was back at NASA flying in the simulators and studying whenever I could find the time. It didn't take long to figure out that this wasn't going to work out very well. I found out that going to medical school wasn't easy, that it was a full-time job and then some. It was too hard to try to do both, and by October, I realized that my time at NASA needed to come to an end. I retired at the end of the month, but even then, I wasn't so sure it was going to help.

As I was still trying to play catch-up, all of the facts I needed to know off the top of my head just weren't there yet. By the end of the first couple of blocks of classes, I was incredibly discouraged and wondered if I had done the right thing. I took it very hard whenever I didn't score well on a test.

I was used to doing well in all my academic endeavors. I had flown four times on board the space shuttle, including the very first mission following the *Challenger* disaster. I wasn't used to—what's the word for it? Oh yes, that's right. I wasn't used to *failure*, but I just couldn't seem to shake the feeling that maybe the grass wasn't greener in medical school after all. Information was coming at me with the force and fury of a fire hose in medical school, and I was depressed about not being able to keep the high standards to which I was accustomed.

For the first time in my life, I came close to quitting. Maybe I could go back to NASA and start flying again. I shared my concerns with fellow astronaut Ellen Baker, who was a doctor. Her response was definitely to the point. *You can't drop out in the first year. I won't allow it.*

Not that I was slacking off before, but I buckled down the best I could and tried to push the doubts out of my

Me hitting the books during medical school.

mind. I wrote down prayers and encouraging Scripture verses to scatter around almost everywhere and, gradually, it began to work. The gap separating myself from classmates who already knew much of the material from their premed classes narrowed, and that helped me gain confidence. By the end of my first full year of medical school, I was back on track.

—‹ ›—

The path I was on became smoother, but it was still headed uphill. While working in the astronaut office, I'd always had a huge variety of responsibilities to juggle. I might train in a simulator for a launch in the morning, on some sort of experiment over lunch if I wasn't at the gym, and in the pool for a simulated spacewalk in the afternoon. Other days I might go flying in a T–38 jet or give a speech at some event. My mind was always shifting gears, which kept things interesting and exciting.

Medical school, on the other hand, was a flat-out grind. I was up most mornings no later than 5:30 a.m., and after starting off with a Scripture reading, I studied on the bus ride to school and during every single free moment I could possibly muster. When I pored over a textbook while on an elliptical machine in the gym, even my workouts became study sessions. I combed through notes while waiting to pick Matt up from his debate tournaments and while at Dan's baseball games. I made it to bed by 11:30 p.m. if I was lucky, only to start the whole routine over again the next morning.

Somewhere along the way, I picked up a nifty, if somewhat painstaking, method of taking notes. After each lecture, I would summarize the main points. Then I would record my summary on a cassette and listen to it over and over ... *and over* ... again, while I was running, driving my car, whatever.

For me, at least, it helped soak what I was trying to learn into my brain. Finally, the first part of medical school, which involved mostly classroom work and labs, was over. The next part, the clinical years, was so

Courtesy of NASA

Me in the rear station of a T-38.

much better for me. Patients and their problems were no longer hypothetical—I was finally getting to see actual patients, people with real-life problems. My age seemed to be an advantage for once. People appeared to trust someone older, even if I was a medical student. When I did my rotations at the Veterans Hospital, I was in my element and could really relate to all the patients with military experience. The logical thinking that I developed in engineering and at NASA also was a great help in figuring out diagnoses and treatment plans.

There were a few moments of levity along the way. I never made a big deal out of my career as an astronaut because I certainly didn't expect or want any special treatment. Some of my professors and most of my fellow students knew of my adventures, while others did not. A visiting attending physician in the medical intensive care unit once began describing the rate at which air leaks from a ventilator, which is a machine that helps patients breathe, who can't do so on their own. He compared it to the leak rate on the space shuttle, and when he did, the percentage he gave was far higher than what it actually was.

Seeing the small grins that were breaking out around the room by the other students and the residents on the team at the mention of the shuttle, I felt compelled to respond.

Excuse me, sir, but the space shuttle doesn't leak nearly that much.

The doctor was taken aback by a medical student with the nerve to question his authority on the matter. He huffed and he puffed, and I thought he was going to blow my house down.

What?! You should never question an attending physician like that! How would you know?

My reply prompted outright laughter from the rest of the team.

Well, sir, I actually flew on board the space shuttle.

—◄ ├►—

A major decision loomed in the year or so before graduation. What kind of doctor did I want to become? Global health was something that I wanted to do—the time I spent overseas in the Marines along with the vistas of Earth from space had cemented that longing in place.

What field of medicine would give me the best skill set to treat all ages of patients, from newborns to the aged? Internal medicine, which deals with the prevention, diagnosis, and treatment of adult diseases, was an option. Another possibility was pediatrics, which is basically the same thing as internal medicine, except in children.

Baylor just so happened to have a combined residency program in internal medicine and pediatrics. Bingo! If I could possibly figure out a way to get into the program, it would literally be the best of two worlds. To avoid disrupting my family, I wanted to remain in Houston. The combined residency would maximize the number of people I could one day help in international medicine. There was only one problem—the residencies usually started in the summer, and I was going to graduate six months earlier in December. I really wanted to stay at Baylor, but how could I work this out?

Dr. Ralph Feigin was the longtime chairman of the pediatrics department, head of the residency program, and a world-renowned expert in infectious disease. He was the godfather of all things pediatric at Baylor, and when he talked, everybody listened. He was a true genius with a photographic memory, the ultimate master of time management who could seemingly juggle a hundred things in the air simultaneously. All the while, he was the kindest man you could imagine.

As the months prior to completion of my medical degree grew shorter, I got a phone call at home one night, and when I answered, I could barely believe my ears. It was Dr. Feigin.

David, you're going to be getting a phone call in a few minutes from a graduate of Harvard Medical School. She is living in Australia now but is going to apply for the pediatrics program here. I would really like to have her join our pediatrics residency program. Could you tell her about Baylor and what we have to offer?

At this point I was really wondering why Dr. Feigin, the one person who knew everything about Baylor pediatrics, would want me, a mere medical student, to talk to her. Before finishing, Dr. Feigin added one more little item of interest.

By the way, her husband wants to be an astronaut. That's why she's interested in coming to Houston.

After saying, "Sure thing, Dr. Feigin," I knew that this was an opportunity that shouldn't be lost. Thinking fast, I came up with a request of my own.

Before you get off the phone, I'd like to do my residency in Med-Peds [internal medicine–pediatrics] here at Baylor beginning in December.

Okay. You've got it.

The short conversation was my residency interview, simple as that. It sure made it easier than paying travel expenses to interview at a bunch of schools around the country, and I could start residency on exactly the day that I wanted. The young woman, Chantal Caviness, came to Baylor and became a stellar resident, pediatric emergency room physician, and researcher. Her husband, Greg Chamitoff, a brilliant engineer, eventually did become an astronaut, who served a sixth-month stint on board the International Space Station. He was also a member of the STS-134 crew, the next-to-last flight in the history of the space shuttle program. Some might say it was chance that our paths crossed, but it was not. It was divine providence!

I can actually say that I really enjoyed those last years of medical school, so much so that I never took any time off or vacation. As a result, I was able to graduate from medical school with honors in December 1995, about five months earlier than the rest of my classmates. One goal had been achieved. I had officially become a doctor.

My residency began the next day.

The slot as an internal medicine and pediatrics resident was mine, and, as usual, I dove headlong into this very challenging four-year program.

You are officially a doctor when you graduate from medical school, but it's basically the same thing as being newly selected as an astronaut but not having flown. Medical school gave us the basic skills, but now we needed to hone them. Residents are now allowed to work just eighty hours a week, but back then, there was no limit. I might be on call every third night, and it wasn't all that unusual to be at the hospital for thirty-six hours or more at a time before coming back and doing the same thing a couple of days later, for months at a time.

Taking the bus stopped being practical when I started my clinical rotations in medical school. In those ancient days before MP3s and podcasts, I listened to cassette tapes featuring current topics in medicine while I was in the car. When I drove home from work in my trusty Toyota Tercel—the one I still own!—I would sometimes doze off at a stoplight after being up for thirty-six hours and wait for the person behind me to honk and awaken me.

I never missed a day of residency due to calling in sick, even though I probably should have stayed home a few times. I really did not want to let my fellow residents down by being gone, and the truth was that I really loved it. Believe it or not, I once had surgery to repair a hernia on a rare day off and then headed right back to work the next day. I was definitely a bit sore while scurrying around the hospital floors that day!

By then, my NASA days seemed like a lifetime ago. Occasionally, however, there would be flashbacks to the past. During my first year of residency, I was doing a rotation on internal medicine at the Veterans Hospital. I was about to do a thoracentesis—a procedure in which excess fluid is drawn off from the space around the lungs—when I received a page. It was from Dr. Bobby Alford, one of the most distinguished surgeons at Baylor and a senior dean at the medical school.

He was in the process of forming a group that would later become the National Space Biomedical Research Institute (NSBRI). It would be a consortium of universities, headed by Baylor, that would look into the multitude of biomedical problems that are present on long-duration manned spaceflights, such as to Mars or to the space station. He wanted me, a lowly intern, to be the chairman of one of the panels that would oversee the activities of the NSBRI!

Dr. Alford is not one of those people you say no to, but I had my hands full both literally and figuratively at that moment! I agreed to do it, although I didn't exactly know where I was going to squeeze it into my already crazy schedule. Although I later stepped down as chairman, I still am a member of this committee, having truly enjoyed staying abreast of the latest developments in space medicine through the years. It has been fulfilling to see how my second (or third) career as a medical doctor has complemented my experience as an astronaut.

Residency was so much different than medical school because it felt like I was finally making a difference in people's lives. I was confident in my capabilities, and it really did not seem like work, although some of the rotations were worse than others from a time standpoint.

One night I was on call in the neonatal intensive care unit when a mother delivered octuplets — eight babies. It's incredibly rare, but rare things were what I came to expect when working in the Texas Medical Center, which is advertised as the largest medical center in the world.

For four years, that was the kind of life that I led. With the end of my residency in 1999, I was a full-fledged, board-eligible internal medicine – pediatrics doctor. Within the next eight months after joining the faculty at Baylor, I passed my board examinations in both pediatrics and internal medicine and was fully certified. My lifelong dream had come true, and now it was time to venture out into the world to lend a helping hand.

Chapter 15

To the Ends of the Earth

HIV—human immunodeficiency virus—causes an insidious infection that attacks the human immune system, and it all too often comes with a stigma that's almost as hard to overcome as the illness itself. When the disease becomes advanced or is associated with certain other diseases, it is called AIDS—acquired immunodeficiency syndrome.

As I was finishing up my residency, the Baylor International Pediatric AIDS Initiative (BIPAI) began to work in conjunction with the Bristol-Myers Squibb Foundation's Secure the Future program in Botswana, a small country in southern Africa. For me, it seemed like a perfect entry point into the future. I was going to be the first of many residents who would do rotations in Africa under the banner of BIPAI.

The journey to Botswana began with a stop-off in New York City at the United Nations Building during a ceremony marking World AIDS Day. I was fortunate enough to sit at a table for lunch with basketball legend Magic Johnson. Soon after, I jumped on an airplane for the sixteen-hour flight from New York to Johannesburg, South Africa, before moving on to Gabarone, Botswana.

The flights were long and tiring, but it was nothing compared to the suffering from HIV/AIDS that I would see in the next few weeks. Witnessing firsthand the daily trials of the families affected by HIV/AIDS really opened my eyes. From the outset, Botswana was a study in contrasts. From far above in the space shuttle, I remembered that most of this country looked parched, with much of its land mass located in the Kalahari Desert; yet, to the north, there were the deep greens of luscious foliage in the Okavanga River delta. The country had also experienced an economic boom, thanks mostly to foreign investments and its own diamond deposits.

Yet the country was ravaged by AIDS. Approximately 35 percent of adults at that time were infected, and an unimaginable 68 percent of childhood deaths were attributable to the disease. At that time, none of the latest drugs to fight HIV/AIDS were available, and I remember feeling very helpless.

Back in Houston, the medical facilities in the Texas Medical Center were spotless and fully staffed and equipped. At Princess Marina Hospital, where I worked during my month-long stay, mothers who had just given birth were sleeping on the floor. Family members were often responsible for feeding and giving medications to their children who were hospitalized, because the nursing staff was overwhelmed.

There were almost no specialists there. Although just a Med-Peds resident in the States, I was helping give chemotherapy treatments to cancer patients in Botswana, a task usually carried out by oncologists. There wasn't space to isolate patients with highly communicable diseases from those with compromised immune systems. Sometimes there would be kids suffering from tuberculosis in the same ward as children with lymphoma.

Just the month before, fourteen children had died in this hospital, twelve of them from AIDS. Losing a patient was always difficult, but in that faraway land, it happened every day, left and right. The tragedy unfolding before me in December 1999 was the first of many heartbreaking situations I have encountered on the mission field, and I'm often asked how I'm able to handle such emotionally difficult events.

Doesn't it get to you?

It was easy to see southern Africa from orbit and wish in an abstract kind of way that I could help, but my feet were now solidly on the ground in that country. In a very real sense, it was time to either put up or shut up. I had held on to the goal of becoming a doctor since my childhood, and although what I was seeing and experiencing wasn't pretty, I was determined to stay the course. I made the decision to join BIPAI as a faculty member and enter the fight against HIV/AIDS in Africa.

I've been able to see many wildlife species on my mission trips!

More than a decade later, I can still close my eyes and picture a tiny four-month-old girl who'd been brought to the hospital by her mother with obvious signs of kwashiorkor, an acute form of childhood malnutrition. Her stomach was grossly distended, her muscles totally wasted, and a dark rash covered her face, arms, and legs.

Without even testing her, we knew that she was positive for HIV. There was little that we could do. It was summer in Botswana, and the heat in the wards was something beyond stifling. Even when rain briefly eased the sweltering temperatures, flies swarmed the rooms.

It's hard to write these words even now, but the sight of her mom attempting to shoo the flies away from the sores that were developing all over her infant's body was truly heartbreaking.

———

Over the next eighteen months, I made five more trips to Africa as well as to Eastern Europe and Latin America with BIPAI. The goal was for Baylor's pediatric AIDS program to set up a series of clinics in Africa following the first one that had been constructed in Romania, and I had been involved in the design process.

There were honest differences of opinion regarding the goals of these clinics, the scope of treatment that would be provided, and their relationship with the host countries. I became convinced that it would be better if I left the group, and while the departure was amicable, it was one of the great disappointments of my life that I was not able to continue with a project in whose ideals I so strongly believed.

Looking back, I would have made the same decision again, but I can also celebrate the wonderful success of this program that now spans the continent of Africa and beyond. It is now the largest provider of pediatric HIV/AIDS care in the world. Still, I had reached another crossroads. First, I was searching for a way to continue my desire to do global health work, and, second, my contract at Baylor would soon expire and I would be without a job. I was continuing to do volunteer work and had made several medical mission trips during these first years on faculty. However, I wanted to have a job in which I could teach, do research, and provide medical care that would help people across the globe.

As God has done so many times for me, he brought the right people into my life at the right time. In this case, two familiar faces solved my problems. The first was Dr. Steve Abrams. Remember how I had been on call the day that the octuplets were delivered? Steve was my attending neonatologist that day. It turned out that Steve was heading up a research project for the Coca-Cola Corporation in which a new micronutrient-fortified drink designed to combat malnutrition in the developing world was going to be tested. He needed someone who had experience in the country where the research was going to be done.

That just happened to be Botswana, where I had spent so much time. I was soon back in the country, working on a large clinical trial of the beverage in schools in Gabarone alongside friends I first met on my initial visit to Princess Marina Hospital. What made it even more perfect was that I was completing a master's degree in public health and needed a thesis project. This clinical trial was the perfect topic for my thesis!

This was the start of a wonderful relationship with Steve's team that continues to this day. Steve has been a wise research partner, mentor, and friend. We have worked together on nutritional research and educational projects that have spanned the globe, including China, Vietnam, Pakistan, Sri Lanka, Thailand, India, the Gambia, South Africa, and Central and South America.

Although the work may not seem as high profile as working with HIV/AIDS, for example, we feel strongly that our projects have touched and improved the lives of a multitude of people across the world, particularly children with malnutrition.

I still needed a "day job" in order to maintain my position as a professor at Baylor. Either that, or I needed to find another job outside Baylor that would allow me enough free time to do this research work with Steve and his team. I began interviewing at other practices in Houston and even talked to like-minded Christian doctors in other parts of the United States who shared my passion for missions and allowed time off to do trips abroad.

My old mentor, Dr. Ralph Feigin, was by that time the president and chief executive officer of the Baylor College of Medicine. He called me over to his office one day. He always seemed to know what was going on and had heard that I was looking for a job elsewhere. After chatting for a few moments, he got to the point and asked me about my plans for the future. When I mentioned that I had already interviewed with a small clinic near my home in Houston, he asked what it would take to keep me at Baylor.

Okay ... I could work at a general pediatric clinic at Texas Children's, be an attending physician for the pediatrics residents in the county hospital a couple of months a year, work in the adult emergency room, and continue to be a supervisor in the Med-Peds residency clinic. I'll teach global health courses to medical students. How about continuing my nutritional

Caring for children with AIDS in Thailand.

research? And mission trips. Could I have some time to do mission trips?

Just like the time a few years prior, when I made my impromptu request for a residency position, Dr. Feigin's response was immediate and generous.

That's great. You've got it. And ... I'll raise your salary.

The offer was one I couldn't refuse. With renewed energy, I was back in the multitasking mode, finishing my master's degree, writing research papers, traveling abroad, teaching, seeing patients, and taking intensive language classes in Spanish (an essential skill for any physician working in Texas).

My jobs with Baylor have changed over the years. I went on to work for a number of years in a clinic for children with special needs and disabilities and in a clinic for adolescents, and I'm now with the internal medicine department as a hospitalist. However my role might have changed, I'm still at Baylor all these years later, and global health remains my passion.

Chapter 16

Not Just Passing Out Pills

There is a face, just like the little girl from Botswana, behind every country I've ever visited as a medical missionary or international researcher.

They're the faces of children and adults whom I've helped, and they're the faces of the people who were lost. Some of the faces are filled with despair and others with complete joy. Every single one reminds me of why I've continued to do this for so long now. It's not about how I've traveled the world and seen more sights than I could ever begin to count. It's not about someone telling me how great a guy I am and getting a pat on the back.

It's not about me at all. The faces are also the benchmark against which all of my trips are measured. The question is a simple one, really.

Did I make a difference?

Washing the feet of a man with an infection.

Some groups might say that thousands of people were seen and treated on a particular mission trip, and while that's certainly admirable, my benchmark has always been to focus on the people whose lives have been truly impacted by God's work through me. Sometimes it's just a couple or maybe even one, sometimes quite a few more. If I can't identify who those people might have been, something's wrong with the way that trip went down.

I want to make sure I'm not just passing out pills, saying, "Have a nice life," and then sending someone on their way. If enough time is spent making sure someone gets what they need, and then following up on it, helping just one person makes the trip worthwhile.

Just one person.

Like the little girl in Botswana.

Like the witch doctor I met in Belize in January 2001.

Like so many others on so many different trips around the world.

—◁▮▷—

Belize is a tiny country located on the northeastern coast of Central America. It is a land of breathtaking beauty, which, along with its wildlife, beautiful beaches, reefs, and Mayan ruins, has made it a popular tourist destination. A far cry from the trendy and gleaming tourist spots, however, are the thatched huts located amid the country's sugar cane fields, jungles, and swamps.

It was in one of those huts that I met Manuel, who just happened to be his village's witch doctor. There were no shrunken heads adorning the walls of his home as I had halfway expected, just a photo or two and a few trinkets here and there. He was very ill, too weak to get up off his cot when I first visited, and his sad and jaundiced eyes rarely met mine when we talked.

After leaving some medicine, I offered to pray for Manuel, and to my surprise, he accepted. By my second visit, his condition had noticeably improved and he was back to eating his favorite meal of black beans, chicken, and rice. We talked, and by my third and final visit, we were friends and something akin to colleagues, who worked hard to fight against the suffering of our patients.

The words he left me with still ring in my ears. In his native language, Manuel told me, "Your medicine is very powerful." He was not referring to the remedies I carried with me in my bag, but to the faith in my heart that I had shared with him. God is so good!

—◄ ┃ ►—

As I look back on the trips I've made, each one is associated with memories that make it special.

When I visited Myanmar in January–February 2003, we could venture no more than three kilometers—a couple of miles or so—from the clinic in which we were working. Armed soldiers watched us very closely. Years later, I would travel to North Korea, arguably the most repressive government in the world. Visiting places such as these has made me appreciate the religious and personal freedoms that we have in the United States, and ever so thankful for the American flag under which I have lived and worked for so long.

About a month after returning from Myanmar, I went to work on a United Nations–sponsored food fortification project in Pakistan. Our intent was to test the effectiveness of a program to fortify wheat flour with iron, a process that has been done in the United States and other developed countries for many years. The hope was that this program would greatly reduce the amount of anemia caused by iron deficiency in Pakistan. On the night of March 1, 2003, I was invited to a birthday party at the home of one of my coworkers in the sprawling city of Rawalapindi. We suddenly heard a lot of commotion going on outside and what seemed like gunfire in the distance. What in the world was happening? The next

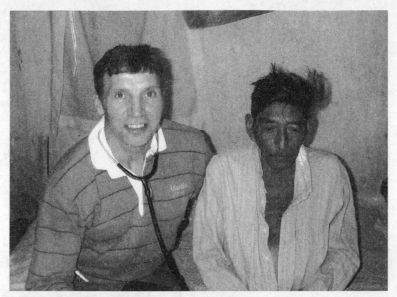

The medicine man in Belize.

morning, we found out. Khalid Sheikh Mohammed, one of the masterminds of the 9/11 terrorist attacks, had been captured by the Pakistani intelligence agency very near where we were at that very moment.

That wasn't the only memorable moment from the trip to Pakistan. One weekend I had the chance to visit the Kashmir area, widely considered one of the most beautiful yet volatile places on the face of the earth, due to disputes over the region between Pakistan and India. There was a conference late in my Pakistan stay in Peshawar, the gateway to the Khyber Pass, the main passageway through the mountains between Pakistan and Afghanistan.

In those delicate days just two weeks before the start of the invasion of Iraq, I was told to dress myself for the conference not as an American, but as a local Pakistani citizen. After the conference, I went to a local shop in Peshawar where the proprietor told me that I looked like I was from Kabul, Afghanistan. I guess the disguise worked.

I still have the outfit.

Chapter 17

An Iraqi Road Trip

Although I had been a member of the United States Marine Corps for twenty years, I never had to fire a rifle in anger. That was fine with me, because as long as I was not doing the shooting, the chances were pretty good that I wasn't going to be in somebody's gunsights!

My streak ended during a trip to Iraq in August 2003, less than six months after the start of the war.

I was on the ground in Basra, Iraq, as part of a joint effort between Mission to the World, the medical arm of the Presbyterian Church in America, and evangelist Pat Robertson's Operation Blessing International. Dictator Saddam Hussein had been toppled from power and an intense search was in progress to find him. Stubborn pockets of resistance remained and organized acts of terror were starting to occur regularly. I knew that this was not the safest place to go, but I had heard reports

The mothers and children of Iraq.

of how desperate ordinary Iraqis were for medical care after all the looting that had taken place, and I jumped at the chance when asked to volunteer.

One night, I walked from the hotel where I was staying over to the United Nations headquarters building so I could use the Internet to write home. An explosion at a liquor store next door shook our building, in what was apparently a terrorist act. A day or two later, a firefight broke out between soldiers and insurgents just as we were leaving the hospital in which we'd been working.

Another night, the people of Basra went out into the streets and fired their guns into the air to celebrate news that Saddam Hussein's sons Oddai and Qusai had been killed. The next morning in the hospital, we helped treat a young boy who had been wounded by one of these bullets returning to Earth the previous night.

Rather than making me want to leave, these experiences made it seem like we were in the right place at the right time, the place where God could put us to good use, where people needed us the most. As an aviator and astronaut, I was no stranger to danger. I certainly wasn't going to go looking for a way to get myself into trouble, but if the risk was acceptable, I wasn't going to shrink away from it, either.

Almost exactly six years later, I once again was caught in gunfire halfway around the world. And as we shall see later, the results were deadly.

—❧—

In Basra, as in most of Iraq, equipment from hospitals had been stripped away, picked clean by looters. In one hospital, doctors patrolled corridors with loaded AK-47s in an attempt to keep anyone from stealing beds, supplies, and whatever else they could get their hands on. Amazingly, at least one medical school was still in session, and when I helped administer final oral exams, students could tell me what a CT scanner was—but they had never actually seen one.

The situation was desperate in many places. Many of those we treated were known as Marsh Arabs—a group left displaced and destitute when Saddam Hussein drained the wetlands in the area between the Tigris and Euphrates Rivers following uprisings in 1991. This group had lived and made their livelihood in this vast sea of tall reeds for thousands of years, and now their delicate habitat, along with their way of life, had been destroyed. We worked for a week in this area. Many images of their suffering are seared into my memory to this day. One pregnant woman, who had already given birth to five children who were all severely developmentally delayed, asked through an interpreter if *this* child was going to be normal.

"What can I do?" she asked through the translator. "What can I do?"

There was no way of knowing whether her child would be healthy, and I muttered, "I don't know if anything can be done."

Although I tried to look away, I caught the look in her eyes as what I'd said filtered through the translator. It struck something deep down inside my soul.

"But I'll try," I replied weakly. It was of no use, however. She left the clinic and I never saw her again. I have always wondered what happened to her, wishing that I would have taken down her name and tried to help her. I resolved never to repeat a false promise again.

—◄►—

While trying to set up another temporary clinic in an Iraqi mosque deep in the marshlands, Danish soldiers tried to keep order at the front door as crowds began to press in on the building. Parents were opening windows and literally throwing their children inside so that they could be seen and treated by one of just two doctors and a medical student.

The village chief was part of the crowd, and he was rather firm in his request to be seen early in the clinic. I asked the medical student to go check on the local dignitary. When he came back a few minutes later, his face was ashen.

Dr. Hilmers, I think I killed the village chief.

What?!

The gentleman was having chest pains, and my young associate had given him a more potent form of the usual nitroglycerin pill. There was only one problem. The dosage was evidently too high for the guy to handle, and he hit the floor, unconscious, with his blood pressure bottoming out.

That's just great, I thought. *Here we are in the middle of a huge, unruly crowd of Iraqis and we've just killed their chief.*

There were no intravenous fluids to give him, so I gently propped his feet up to get blood flowing to his head, gave him small sips of water, and hoped for the best. Fortunately, he came around and survived.

The village chief made it out of his encounter with an American medical student in relatively good shape, just like some friends and I following an impromptu weekend journey through southeastern Iraq.

It all began when someone decided that we should visit Abraham's birthplace in the ancient city of Ur. Without a doubt whatsoever, it was one of the craziest things I've ever done, but five or six of us hopped into a car and took off for a four- or five-hour, unescorted journey from Basra to Ur.

Road trip!

On the way out, we were stopped by an Air Force sentry who asked who we were and where we were going. The look on his face when we told him said it all. *You really shouldn't be doing this.*

God was watching out for us. We never made it inside Ur, as it was put off limits by the military to prevent looting. We did get close enough to clearly see the Great Ziggurat of Ur, dating back to the sixth century BC and reconstructed by Saddam Hussein on the original site in the 1980s.

Before we headed "home," we stopped and knocked on the door of a hut located on the outskirts of the central marshlands. When an interpreter explained that we had food to share, the group was invited inside. Although they were hospitable, it didn't take much to figure out that at least one of our hosts wasn't impressed by our white-bread sandwiches.

He spit it out, not liking the taste!

In the third chapter of Genesis, God ordered Adam and Eve to neither touch nor eat from a particular tree in the Garden of Eden. They did so anyway after being tempted by a serpent—Satan. Legend has it that the garden paradise was located in Al Qurnah, Iraq, near where the Tigris and Euphrates Rivers come together. The tree? It's there, too, at least according to locals.

As I stood there looking at the tree, where mankind first fell into sin, I couldn't have imagined that the upcoming year would be one of the most difficult of my life. I was about to be broken in both body and spirit.

Chapter 18

Sin and Redemption

I should have died on the side of that mountain, and had it not been for desperately flailing about and catching hold of a branch on my way down, I have no doubt whatsoever that I would have.

Machu Picchu, located in the mountains of Peru, is widely believed to have been built in the fifteenth century as an estate for the Incan emperor Pachacuti. Most people visit by taking the train to a town near the river below and then taking a bus to the ruins. The more adventuresome get off the train early and make the multi-day trek along what is known as the Inca Trail to reach the entrance to the city.

The day after I arrived was wet and misty and the ruins were surrounded in fog. Hoping for some cool photographs and for the clouds to clear during my March 2004 trip to the mountain, I made the climb up a steep peak overlooking the city only to find that a mist was still enveloping the entire area. The weather cleared on my way back down, so I returned up the very narrow and steep path. After snapping my photos at the summit, just after I started a second descent, my foot slipped on a rock.

I slid down the steep slope for 200 feet or more, rocks, pebbles, and sticks tearing at my clothes and flesh every inch of the way. Miraculously, a branch arrested my fall. Once I regained my senses, I went into "ER doctor mode" and took stock of my body. It didn't take much to figure out that both bones in my lower left leg and my left ankle were broken very badly. I took my belt off and grabbed a couple of branches to form a make-shift splint. There wasn't much anyone nearby could do to help on the jagged cliff, and the path up was too narrow, so I was forced to basically scoot down on my own until I reached a lower level where a rescue party could meet me.

Strangely enough, I don't remember being in any pain, although it sure looked bad. Later that night, I was treated in Cuzco, the closest large city, about three hours away, and passed out when my fracture was set in place. When I woke up the next morning, I was still in the clothes I'd had on while climbing ... and falling. My shirt was one that I'd worn during the flight of STS-26! Believe it or not, the man who drove the ambulance to pick me up at the train station in Cuzco also helped the doctor set my leg, and when I woke up in the morning, he was also sweeping the floors near the bed where I was lying. It was time to get back to Houston!

My view from the top of the Inca trail right before I fell.

Two days later, I arrived in Houston and checked into a hospital. After two surgeries, my doctor told me I probably should never run again. An athlete in both high school and college, I'd continued to run throughout my adult life. I'd even made it a point to get a few miles in as soon as possible after each of my shuttle flights, most of the time within hours of landing. The doctor was right, but only to a certain extent. I wouldn't run every day.

I now run every *other* day.

—⊷—

Despite my injuries, I should have been giving thanks for the preservation of my life and the fulfillment of so many dreams. Medical school and residency were behind me. I was doing what I loved and had always imagined.

This should have been the best time of my life, but restlessness had taken root in my soul. Somehow I wasn't satisfied with all that God had given me. Instead of getting on my knees and thanking God for what he had done in my life, I let pride and a desire for more get in my way. As I brooded, my family life deteriorated. I neglected to do the things that God most expects from a Christian—to be obedient to his will, to be a good husband and father. As too often happens these days, my marriage of thirty years ended in divorce a year later.

How could I have been so disobedient? I had a family who had stuck with me when I was either away or equally distant, locked in my room studying or working on some project. God had seen me through many years of hazardous adventures. When I had the chance to make the right choice and obey God, I turned away from the One who had never failed me.

God did not abandon me. Certainly, he chastised me during that year and beyond. Sometimes I became depressed to the point of despair, feeling a guilt and unworthiness beyond what I ever could have imagined.

Attending to a woman in Nepal.

At times it was difficult to even get up in the morning to go to work.

I can understand the despair that King David encountered due to his sin, and later his sense of gratitude for God's mercy. The good news for me, for King David, and for each of us, however, is that sin is not the victor. Despite its terrible effects, the Bible says in 1 John 1:9, "If we confess our sins, [God] is faithful and just and will forgive us our sins and purify us from all unrighteousness."

Little by little, my prayers were answered and the cloud began to lift. Although there was a period in which I was reluctant to go on medical mission trips,

I made a few here and there, including one to Nepal. When a Christmas Eve 2004 earthquake and tsunami killed more than a quarter of a million people, a group of us from Mission to the World spent two weeks the following month in a Sri Lankan refugee camp providing medical and spiritual care to those who were left homeless or had lost loved ones during the tsunami.

All the suffering and the grief that I saw there once again helped me to realize how fortunate I really was. We lived in tents in the camp along with all the other refugees—as well as snakes and elephants—and endured the hardships and primitive conditions along with them. The fellowship and experiences that I shared with the team helped me immensely.

Being placed on a pedestal just because I flew in space once upon a time has always been awkward for me, but I can assure you that I have never been perfect. That was the case before my divorce, and it has been the case afterward. At the end of the day, we're all the same at the foot of the cross—the astronaut and the floor sweeper, the pastor and the criminal, the prince and the pauper.

The important thing is that we decide once and for all to learn from our mistakes. To help do that, there's a lot of comfort to be found in the Bible. Sometimes the hardest thing for us to do is to really believe that God, through the sacrifice of his Son, can absolve us of our guilt. Somehow I could not believe that God could truly forgive me, and thus I refused to forgive myself.

It wasn't until I took God at his word that I could move on. Each of my four space shuttle missions was

Tsunami victim in Sri Lanka.

based on engineering and science, but I found that the answer to the problem of sin must be based on faith. I'd never been more thankful for that fact as I began to get back on my feet. A wiser and more thankful person emerged as a result of this difficult time.

Chapter 19

Closest Call

The trip didn't get off to a great start, and it only got worse — far worse — from there.

While I was still serving as an associate professor at the Baylor College of Medicine, one of my former Med-Peds residents was married to a pastor at a local Presbyterian congregation here in Houston. When the church put together a mission to San Salvador, El Salvador, in August 2009, I joined the group to help provide medical care.

The problems started as soon as we hit the ground in the country, when box after box of the medical supplies we had gathered were confiscated at the airport. That forced us to make do with whatever we'd brought along in our own luggage, and it wasn't much.

Located on the outskirts of the country's capital city, the church in which our clinic was organized was tiny, maybe the size of several average rooms. The first day went well enough. The church had, for all intents and purposes, adopted a local man, allowing him to sleep in the building. He set up some loudspeakers and announced that the church was open to any and all comers for free medical care.

On the second day of the clinic, he stood close by as I examined a patient in the crowded room with my stethoscope. Suddenly I noticed out of the corner of my eye that people were scattering. Quickly glancing up, I saw a man wearing a mask, probably from a local gang, firing into the room with a pistol. My new friend, the homeless man who'd made all the announcements over the loudspeakers, had been shot in the chest. The woman I was examining was hit in her leg.

Has anyone else been hit?!

Almost everyone had already scattered and was running through a side entrance. Me? Because I had the stethoscope in my ears, I was one of the last to notice what was going on and briefly met eyes with the masked gunman. I hit the ground in a classic Marine Corps belly crawl, trying to figure out what to do next. I couldn't stand up and run, or I surely would've been hit in the back. Could I somehow stop the shooter? I kept as low as I could, scrambled out of the room as fast as possible, and reentered when the firing stopped. I saw that the shooter had vanished.

I ran to the most seriously wounded victim, the homeless man, now with a clean wound through his heart. He was still alive, but just barely. I tried to close my eyes and pretend that I was back in the ER in Houston. I did CPR while at the same time trying to somehow staunch the flow of blood, but it was of no use.

He died right there on the floor of that tiny little church-turned-medical-clinic.

It turned out that my other patient had a minor wound in the ankle to which I quickly attended. Miraculously, no one else was hit. When the police arrived a few minutes later, they didn't ask any questions about who did what and where. Gathering evidence seemed to be of little, if any, importance to them. Their only advice was to leave the area, which turned out to be one of the deadliest in the world the following year. To put it into perspective, according to statistics from the United Nations, there were fourteen violent deaths per 100,000 people in war-torn Iraq in 2010.

There were seventy-one violent deaths per 100,000 people in El Salvador during that same time period. To the police, my friend was just another homeless guy who'd been in the wrong place at the wrong time.

Chapter 20

Dad

When any natural disaster strikes, there's almost always a scramble to line up travel plans and get on the scene to help out. It was no different following a devastating earthquake that leveled much of Haiti, a small island country located just off the eastern tip of Cuba, on January 12, 2010.

I had been involved in a number of disaster relief situations before, including other earthquakes such as the one that devastated the town of Pisco, Peru, in 2007. Of course I wanted to go and lend a hand. The problem was that the airport in the capital of Port-au-Prince was so saturated with flights bringing in supplies and emergency teams that it was difficult to find a flight into the country. I thought I had one flight two days after the earthquake, but after I'd swapped commitments in four different hospitals and clinics in Houston, the plans fell through.

I'd worked with Project Medishare, a charitable organization affiliated with the University of Miami, in Haiti on a medical mission just the summer before, but the group did not have a seat for me on a plane. Baylor began the process of putting a team together as well, but that too was moving along very slowly. About a week later, I received an email from my friends on the disaster relief team at Mission to the World—the crew with whom I'd made the trips to Iraq and Sri Lanka. They were lining up a team and would be heading out soon; would I like to go? You bet! The flight they had arranged was going to leave out of Chicago, so not only would I be able to get to Haiti, I would also be able to visit my dad.

Mom passed away on October 23, 2002, in DeWitt. Dad was in declining health when he was moved in October 2009 to be near my sister, Ginny, and her husband, Jack, in Evanston, Illinois, just a stone's throw north of Chicago. I flew in early from Houston to Chicago, and Ginny picked me up at the airport. We went to see Dad that evening before I had to catch a late-night hop down to Haiti. Although Dad was suffering from Alzheimer's disease, he was as lucid as I had seen him in a long time. We chatted and reminisced for a couple of hours before I had to leave. I left his room in the nursing home, thinking that it had been a really, really good visit.

I never saw him again.

Dad and me on the farm.

On February 1, 2010, just two or three days after I touched down in Haiti, the news arrived that Dad had passed away. There was really no decision to be made about returning to the States, because he did not want a funeral or a service, just cremation. Besides, transportation back home wasn't readily available. I stayed in Haiti for my entire two-week tour of duty, and months later we scattered Dad's ashes over one of his favorite spots, on a bluff overlooking the Mississippi River. I was ever so thankful that God, in his perfect timing, had arranged for me to see Dad one more time before he passed away.

As with the tragic earthquake and tsunami that struck Indonesia on Christmas Eve 2004 and killed untold thousands of people, it's equally as hard to put into words the catastrophe that was unfolding in Haiti. The initial earthquake was measured at a magnitude of 7.0, with more than fifty aftershocks causing further damage in the following days. Thousands died, while a staggering one million people or more were left homeless. Like most buildings in the capital, the presidential palace was in ruins.

Such numbers are so hard to comprehend, they can sometimes seem like some sort of abstract concept — that many people couldn't be injured in the same place at the same time, could they? They could, and they were.

My small group found a hospital that, while damaged and unsafe for patients to stay inside, still had some facilities that were in relatively good shape. We asked the remaining staff members if they could use some help, and their response was both immediate and emphatic.

Yes!

A group of French medical workers was staying at the French embassy, which meant that they could only arrive at nine o'clock every morning and had to leave around four in the afternoon, leaving us to handle the large number of patients on our own for the rest of the day and night. Neonatology — the care of newborn children, especially those who are sick or premature — constituted a significant part of my pediatric residency (remember the octuplets?), but I hadn't had too many opportunities to practice it since then. In that hospital in Haiti, however, I had little choice. There were a lot of deliveries, some of which we did ourselves, and I was the only pediatrician. Many of the newborns were either premature, in serious need of medical care particularly with breathing problems, or both.

As always, one case sticks in my memory. Like a lot of the new deliveries, one newborn should've been in a neonatal intensive care unit, but even before the earthquake, these were few and far between in Haiti. He could not breathe on his own, and so we placed a tiny breathing tube into his trachea, the pipe through which air is brought into the lungs. A bag was connected to the tube and, when squeezed, pumped air into his tiny lungs. We tried calling other hospitals, hoping to find one that had adequate facilities to treat him. There were none.

We loaded him into an ambulance and drove to various places in the dead of the night, still squeezing the bag to breathe for him, still trying to get him the help he needed. One place was a no-go, then another. The Navy's USS *Comfort* hospital ship was just off the coast, but one arranged meeting place at a dock fell through. After five or six hours of desperately trying to find the child some help and "bagging" him all the way, we finally met up with a Navy pediatrician from the *Comfort* who was able to take him from the dock to the ship.

The boy died a few days later.

—◄ ►—

Many times, the problem in Haiti was not a lack of supplies but rather a lack of organization and infrastructure.

The Haiti earthquake made for makeshift hospitals in the streets.

The quakes damaged communications and distribution facilities across the country, and many roads throughout the city were impassable. Those issues and many more combined to make a bad situation even worse.

Plenty of medicines were pouring in from all over the world, but it would all too often just be dumped on the doorstep of a treatment center without any kind of real inventory. If I had a minute, I would just start rummaging through piles of supplies to see what was actually there.

On top of that, there was virtually no place to put everyone who needed our help and nowhere for them to go afterward. Our "emergency room," if it could be called that, was outdoors with only a sea of tents to shelter those who were receiving treatment or who had no other place to recuperate after an amputation or other major surgery. With so many cases pouring in, it was all but impossible to follow up with a patient once he or she was treated and stabilized.

On duty for sixteen to eighteen hours every day, I cannot remember ever being that tired. The hospital was hit with wave after wave of patients, all frantically seeking assistance. This wasn't just the front lines of a battlefield. Instead, it seemed at times that we served as the *only* line of defense these people had. I had been placed here for a reason, and I was going to do my job to the best of my ability.

Just keep going, I told myself.

Just keep going.

Epilogue

Although my last mission was more than twenty years ago, my time at NASA is something that's never too far from my mind in one way or another. I don't spend much free time dwelling on the space program, but there are countless triggers to remind me of all those adventures. Somebody might ask me about the latest news on the space program or just inquire about my experiences long ago. It might be a youngster writing me about a school project that he's doing on space who has a few questions.

It might be a friend giving me a good-natured ribbing about still wearing shirts I wore on board the space shuttle twenty-five years ago. They're just shirts. But to my friend, they're shirts that were *flown in space*. There is, evidently, a difference.

There's a photo of the Houston area taken from the shuttle that hangs just inside my front door. Most of the time, I don't even notice it as I pass by. But when I do, the memories it brings back sweep across the stages of my life. I'm reminded of the views of Earth I saw from orbit, and then I recall those same places as I stood on the ground working as a medical missionary and researcher.

I remember those wonderful times on the shuttle, looking out the overhead window as the Earth rotated beneath us. Sometimes when the flight plan would call for us to be sleeping, I would wake up and float upstairs to the windows from the lower deck. There would be this magnificent feeling of solitude with only the hum of the cabin fans to remind me that I was not floating here alone in the universe. As the shuttle traveled through the dark phase of our orbit, I would look outside and feel like I was in a small boat bobbing in a vast sea of stars. There was an overwhelming feeling of the awesome greatness of God, the Maker and Creator of this amazingly complex universe. It reminded me of how much we need his presence in our lives to survive and how he calls us to care for our fellow inhabitants of this tiny speck in the cosmos that we call Earth.

I'm reminded of trips you've read about in this book, and many more that you haven't. I saw Vietnam from 200 miles up, and recalled that the war there was one of the most divisive issues of my generation in high school and college. I go there quite often, serving with a United Nations food fortification project and Hope Initiative, a Houston-based group devoted to poverty reduction, child development, and community enrichment programs in the country. I started my journey with the Marines as the war raged on in Vietnam. What I have learned is that while the long years of war could not solve the disputes between our countries, understanding, economic cooperation, mutual respect, and perhaps a bit of love have gone a long way to heal bitter wounds.

I am reminded of two college campuses at which I have spoken—the Yanbian University of Science and Technology (YUST) in China and the Pyongyang University of Science and Technology (PUST) in North Korea—where dedicated Christian educators train local students. YUST was founded in 1992, while classes at PUST started in 2010. The fact that these schools even exist is nothing short of a miracle, especially in the isolated nation of North Korea.

Could PUST possibly help open doors to diplomacy where veiled—and outright—military threats over the last sixty years have failed? That's my fervent prayer, and when I think of various exchanges I have had with students there, I'm optimistic that it is one that will someday be answered.

I think of a recent mission trip to Ethiopia, where I journeyed with a group from Citylife Presbyterian Church in Boston. They turned out to be wonderful spirit-filled travel companions, and their passion for the Lord underscored their commitment to the patients we were seeing, most of whom were HIV positive. During home visits, we saw the sobering conditions in which they lived.

Through it all, the memories help me to remember the lessons of the past and to strive to make the world as beautiful a place to live as it appeared from space many years ago.

The memories also sustain and drive me at home in Houston. Although I'm well over sixty years old now, I'm as busy as I've ever been. That's just the way I like it — I don't know what I'd do if I didn't have a lot of irons in the fire at any given time!

I serve as an associate professor in Baylor College of Medicine's departments of pediatrics and internal medicine, and am also part of the Center for Space Medicine. I continue to teach, spend a great deal of my time taking care of sick patients in the hospital, and also oversee our group of current Med-Peds residents at a local community clinic. Here's how things can come full circle — Ron Grabe and I flew in space twice together, and years later, I worked with his daughter while she was a med student at Baylor. How cool is that?

Houston's Ben Taub General Hospital is one of the busiest trauma centers in the country, treating more than 100,000 people a year. The vast majority of the patients we see have no health insurance, but their needs are real. It's a fascinating place to work. The people are for the most part truly appreciative of the help we provide, and the variety of cases we see is almost beyond belief. As many of our patients are immigrants from other countries, we see many tropical diseases that one would not expect to encounter here.

Sadly, because they're uninsured, many wait far too long to come in for treatment. So Ben Taub sees many people who are in the very last stage of their lives. Still, it's one more reason to like the job—there is no time in one's life when a patient is in so much need of spiritual and emotional support. Ben Taub and the family shelters in Houston at which I also volunteer are just about as close to doing global missions work as is possible here in the United States.

I remain involved in the National Space Biomedical Research Institute, where we're looking into the physiological barriers to long-term spaceflight such as bone and muscle loss, radiation, and psychological problems. The plan is for space travelers to someday go to Mars, and when the day finally arrives that mankind is ready to set off on that historic journey, we want to make sure that we have provided as much protection as possible for the first Martian explorers. While I won't be privileged to be a part of that first crew, there are still *a lot* of places I saw from the shuttle that I want to see for myself firsthand. And by God's grace, I will.

I would never be one to say that I have had a life "well lived"; I have made too many mistakes for that. What would be more appropriate is to say that I have had a life "well blessed." If you count the number of times in this book where it appears that God has directly intervened in my life, there is no doubt that the latter statement is true. How else could a pretty average guy from a small Midwestern town have been able to participate in so much?

I've been blessed to have two wonderful sons and now two handsome grandsons. Dan and Matt have not followed in their father's footsteps, but I'm relieved that they have not. Like each of us, they have had their own trials in life, yet I could not be more proud of them. Dan and his wife, Amy, worked for a number of years as missionaries in Belarus, a country where religious persecution still exists. They recently returned to the US, and Dan is now studying in seminary. Matt is the "go-to" guy for any kind of technology questions that we may have and has been actively involved in restaurant management.

I have learned why God wants us to have a servant's heart. Not only does this attitude benefit the recipients of our service, but it changes our outlook on life. Whenever I find that my work as a physician has become tiresome or mundane, I know that I need an attitude adjustment and need to think of whom I'm here to serve and who sent me in the first place. As soon as I remember that, my spirit lightens, my resolve returns, and the joy of being a healer is revived. Having a servant's heart (see chapter two of the Book of Philippians) makes all the difference between having a joy-filled life and simply going through the motions.

I've learned to believe in God's promises and power, particularly with regard to forgiveness. In so doing, when I stumble, I am assured of his love and can forgive myself. But God always asks us to strive in the midst of life's difficulties and to use every gift that he has given us. I believe he wants us to have high personal and spiritual goals and to dream to do great things. If he is with us, who can be against us? And then who knows what you can achieve?

I hadn't had much contact with Mike Lounge in years.

After joining NASA as astronaut candidates together, the two of us had trained side by side for hours on end for the flights of STS-61F—which, in the wake of the *Challenger* accident, never actually took place—and STS-26. When our careers in the astronaut office were over, however, we went our separate ways. While I went into medicine, Mike worked for the aerospace company Spacehab and then later for Boeing.

In early 2011, a mutual friend told me that Mike was in St. Luke's Episcopal Hospital, very near Ben Taub Hospital here in the Texas Medical Center. I always passed St. Luke's on my bike ride home from work, so I stopped by one day to check on my friend and colleague.

Every day for more than a week, I visited Mike and tried to help out with his care when and where I could. There was only so much I or anyone else could do, because Mike was suffering from a particularly aggressive cancer. He'd been apparently healthy in January, but on March 1, 2011, my friend and former crewmate passed away.

Nearly a quarter of a century had passed since we'd been named to the crew of STS-26, but Mike's death brought our friendship full circle. I became a doctor, and when our paths crossed again decades after our flight, I was able to help support him and his family. To me, it was one more affirmation that I had made the right decision to spend those long years in medical school and residency. I hadn't squandered the opportunities God placed before me, and that allowed me to help Mike cross the river from this life into the next.

Dick Richards, another 1980 astronaut classmate, sent out an email after Mike's funeral. In it, he said one of the kindest things anybody has ever said about me.

Our own Dr. Dave Hilmers works in the Texas Medical Center and visited Mike frequently. Dave provided valuable counseling to Mike as his condition deteriorated. We should all be so lucky to have someone like Dave who will provide straight talk in this kind of moment.

In all honesty, that's how I want to be remembered. Not as an aviator, engineer, or astronaut, and not as a doctor, but simply as someone who tried to serve others.